Praise for Mark Richard's

HOUSE OF PRAYER NO. 2

"Richard is a fiercely gifted writer. . . . [His] special childhood results in considerable powers of observation, empathy and imagination." —*The New York Times Book Review*

"Amazing. . . . You'll know just after two pages of Richard's effortlessly killer prose that he's special all right. . . . Grade: A." —*Entertainment Weekly*

"Entrancing. . . . Where other memoirists—evangelical and/or literary—just bluff and brag, he makes art." —*The Christian Science Monitor*

"Mark Richard's memoir, *House of Prayer No. 2*, is the finest book he's ever written. No one writes like him. His prose style is both hammerblow and shrapnel. He has written the book of his life." —Pat Conroy

"A lyrical distillation of observations from Richard's boyhood in and out of southern charity hospitals to his becoming a writer and father in search of faith." —*Vanity Fair*

"Hauntingly beautiful. . . . A quintessentially American story." —*Minneapolis Star Tribune*

"A surreal and poetic memoir about faith, self-discovery and forming an artistic inner life."
—*The Free Lance-Star* (Fredericksburg, VA)

"A humorous and heartfelt memoir, never tedious and often lyrical." —*Richmond Times-Dispatch*

"This book is the extraordinary story of a special child who grew up to be a writer, and who may yet—I'm guessing—become a preacher or a priest. There are similar life stories in the South and elsewhere. But few will be written with Richard's powerful talent, his genius." —Clyde Edgerton, *Garden & Gun*

"Gritty and engrossing. . . . His is an account, at times exquisite, of a youth laced with pain, surgeries, body casts, beatings, fear, drinking, isolation, rebellion. With flashes of brilliance. With mysticism and the supernatural and strokes of what many would call luck. . . . An interesting, well-crafted narrative girded with compassion and feeling, this is a good read."
—*The Virginian-Pilot*

"Lovely. . . . Richard captures what is often misunderstood about the Southerner's intimate parlay with God. Appearances to the contrary, it is not about certainty. . . . A fascinating journey."
—*The Oregonian*

"Hot damn! And Glory be! Both. This is a wonderful book."
—Roy Blount, Jr.

"Supremely animated. . . . [Richard's] spiritual journey, conducted in fits and starts and finally claimed in gorgeous hosannas of prose, forms the book's narrative DNA." —*Elle*

"Richard's story is inspirational not because of conventional redemption or simple answers to his struggle, but because he is so honest about both his doubt and his openness to a wide variety of God's manifestations."
—Darcey Steinke, *Los Angeles Review of Books*

"Affecting. . . . Fans who have been waiting to hear from him ever since [*Charity*] won't be disappointed with his new memoir, which sees the welcome return of Richard's charismatic prose style." —*The Atlanta Journal-Constitution*

"The precision of the descriptions is marvelous in this memoir of growing up with infirmity. The depth of Richard's heart is profound, exhilarating, frightening, instructive. *House of Prayer No. 2* is a work of high art." —Rick Bass

"Mark Richard says important things about finding one's way, about love in action, about being a father, and he does so with the precision and grace of an artisan from another time. This is some of the finest writing you will ever read." —Amy Hempel

"If Mark Richard could not write, you could not read this. Since he can, you can't not read it. It is unreal, and Mr. Richard has the wit to make it real." —Padgett Powell

MARK RICHARD

HOUSE OF PRAYER No. 2

Mark Richard is the author of two award-winning short story collections, *The Ice at the Bottom of the World* and *Charity*, and the novel *Fishboy*. His short stories and journalism have appeared in *The New York Times*, *The New Yorker*, *Harper's*, *Esquire*, and *GQ*. He is the recipient of the PEN/Hemingway Award, a National Endowment for the Arts fellowship, and a Whiting Foundation Writer's Award. He lives in Los Angeles with his wife and their three sons.

ALSO BY MARK RICHARD

The Ice at the Bottom of the World

Fishboy

Charity

HOUSE OF PRAYER No. 2

HOUSE OF PRAYER No. 2

A WRITER'S JOURNEY HOME

MARK RICHARD

Anchor Books
A Division of Random House, Inc.
New York

FIRST ANCHOR BOOKS EDITION, FEBRUARY 2012

A portion of this work was originally published in *The Southern Review*
(Autumn, 2011).

The Library of Congress has cataloged the Nan A. Talese/
Doubleday edition as follows:
Richard, Mark, 1955–
House of prayer No. 2 / Mark Richard. —1st American ed.
p. cm.
1. Richard, Mark, 1955– 2. Authors, American—20th century—Biography. I. Title.
PS3568.I313Z46 2011
813'.54—dc22
2010006317

Anchor ISBN: 978-1-4000-7777-9

www.anchorbooks.com

Printed in the United States of America
10 9 8 7 6 5 4 3 2 1

to my father

for my sons

And Jacob awaked out of his sleep, and he said,

Surely the LORD is in this place; and I knew it not.

—GENESIS 28:16

HOUSE OF PRAYER No. 2

SAY YOU HAVE A "SPECIAL CHILD," which in the South means one between Down's and dyslexic. Birth him with his father away on Army maneuvers along East Texas bayous. Give him his only visitor in the military hospital his father's father, a sometime railroad man, sometime hired gun for Huey Long with a Louisiana Special Police badge. Take the infant to Manhattan, Kansas, in winter, where the only visitor is a Chinese peeping tom, little yellow face in the windows during the cold nights. Further frighten the mother, age twenty, with the child's convulsions. There's something "different" about this child, the doctors say.

Move the family to Kirbyville, Texas, where the father cruises timber in the big woods. Fill the back porch with things the father brings home: raccoons, lost bird dogs, stacks of saws, and machetes. Give the child a sandbox to play in, in which scorpions build nests. Let the mother cut the grass and run over rattlesnakes, shredding them all over the yard. Make the mother cry and miss her mother. Isolate her from the neighbors because

she is poor and Catholic. For playmates, give the child a mongol-
oid girl who adores him. She is the society doctor's child and is
scared of thunder. When it storms, she hides, and only the special child can find her. The doctor's wife comes to the house in
desperation. Please help me find my daughter. Here she is, in the
culvert, behind a bookcase, in a neighbor's paper tepee. Please
come to a party, the doctor's wife sniffs, hugging her daughter.
At the party, it goes well for the nervous mother and the forester
father until their son bites the arm of a guest and the guest goes to
the hospital for stitches and a tetanus shot. The special child can
give no reason why.

Move the family to a tobacco county in Southside Virginia.
It is the early sixties, and black families still get around on mule
and wagon. Corn grows up to the backs of houses even in town.
Crosses burn in yards of black families and Catholics. Crew cut
the special child's hair in the barbershop where all the talk is
of niggers and nigger-lovers. Give the child the responsibility
of another playmate, the neighbor two houses down, Dr. Jim.
When Dr. Jim was the child's age, Lee left his army at Appomattox. When Dr. Jim falls down between the corn rows he is always
hoeing, the child must run for help. Sometimes the child just
squats beside Dr. Jim sprawled in the corn and listens to Dr. Jim
talking to the sun. Sometimes in the orange and grey dusk when
the world is empty, the child lies in the cold backyard grass and
watches the thousands of starlings swarm Dr. Jim's chimneys, and
the child feels like he is dying in an empty world.

The child is five years old.

Downstairs in the house the family shares is a rough redneck,

a good man who brought a war bride home from Italy. The war
bride thought the man was American royalty because his name
was Prince. Prince was just the man's name. The Italian war bride
is beautiful and has borne two daughters, the younger is the special
child's age. The elder is a teenager who will soon die of a blood
disease. The beautiful Italian wife and the special child's mother
smoke Salems and drink Pepsi and cry together on the back steps.
They both miss their mothers. In the evening Prince comes home
from selling Pontiacs, and the forester father comes home from
the forest, and they drink beer together and wonder about their
wives. They take turns mowing the grass around the house.

The company the father works for is clearing the land of
trees. The father finds himself clearing the forests off the old
battlefields from the Civil War. The earthworks are still there, stuff
is still just lying around. He comes home with his pockets full of
minié balls. He buys a mine detector from an Army surplus store,
and the family spends weekends way deep in the woods. One
whole Sunday the father and the mother spend the day digging
and digging, finally unearthing a cannon-sized piece of iron agate.
The mother stays home after that. On Sunday nights she calls
her mother in Louisiana and begs to come home. No, her mother
says. You stay. She says this in Cajun French.

THE LITTLE GIRL DOWNSTAIRS is named Debbie. The special
child and Debbie play under the big pecan tree where the corn
crowds the yard. One day the special child makes nooses and
hangs all of Debbie's dolls from the lower limbs of the tree.

Debbie runs crying inside. Estelle, the big black maid, shouts from the back door at the special child to cut the baby dolls down, but she doesn't come out in the yard to make him do this and he does not. She is frightened of the special child, and he knows this. If he concentrates hard enough, he can make it rain knives on people's heads.

Maybe it would be best if something were done with the special child. The mother and father send him to kindergarten across town, where the good folk live. The father has saved his money and has bought a lot to build a house there, across from the General Electric Appliance dealer. Because he spent all his money on the lot, the father has to clear the land himself. He borrows a bulldozer from the timber company and "borrows" some dynamite. One Saturday he accidentally sets the bulldozer on fire. One Sunday he uses too much dynamite to clear a stump and cracks the foundation of the General Electric Appliance dealer's house. The father decides not to build in that neighborhood after all.

In the kindergarten in that part of town there are records the teacher whom the special child calls Miss Perk lets him play over and over. When the other kids lie on rugs for their naps, she lets him look at her books. During reading hour he sits so close to her that she has to wrap him in her arms while she holds the book. The best stories are the ones Miss Perk tells the class herself. About the little girl whose family was murdered on a boat and the criminals tried to sink the boat. The little girl saw water coming in the portholes, but she thought the criminals were just mopping the decks and doing a sloppy job. Miss Perk told about the car wreck she saw that was so bloody she dropped a pen on the floor of her car for her son to fetch so he wouldn't have to see the man with the top of his head ripped off like he had been scalped. On Fridays is Show-and-Tell, and the special child always brings the same thing in for Show-and-Tell, his cat Mr. Priss. Mr. Priss is a huge, mean tomcat that kills other cats and only lets the special child near him. The special child dresses Mr. Priss in Debbie's baby doll clothes, especially a yellow raincoat and yellow sou'wester-style rain hat. Then the special child carries Mr. Priss around for hours in a small suitcase. When his mother asks if he has the cat in the suitcase again, the special child always says, *No, ma'am.*

Miss Perk says the way the other children follow the special child around, that the special child will be something someday, but she doesn't say what.

The father and the mother meet some new people. There is a new barber and his wife. The new barber plays the guitar in the kitchen and sings *Smoke! Smoke! Smoke that cigarette!* He is handsome and wears so much oil in his hair that it stains the sofa when he throws back his head to laugh. He likes to laugh a lot. His wife teaches the mother how to dance, how to do the Twist. There is another new couple in town, a local boy, sort of a black sheep, from country folk, who went away to Southeast Asia to be a flight surgeon and is back with his second or third wife, nobody knows for sure. At the reckless doctor's apartment, they drink beer and do the Twist and listen to Smothers Brothers albums. They burn candles stuck in Chianti bottles. The special child is always along because there is no money for a babysitter and Estelle will not babysit the special child. One night the special child pulls down a book off the doctor's shelf and begins to slowly read aloud from it. The party stops. It is a college book about chemicals. In two more months the child will start first grade.

⁂

AT FIRST, FIRST GRADE IS EMPTY. Most of the children are bringing in the tobacco harvest. The ones who show up are mostly barefoot and dirty and sleep with their heads on the desk all day. A lot of them have fleas and head lice. Most of them have been up all night tying tobacco sticks, their hands are stained black with nicotine.

At first, first grade makes no sense to the special child. The child wants to get to the books, but the books are for later, the teacher tells him. *You must learn the alphabet first.* But the child has learned the alphabet already; Miss Perk taught him the letters perched in her lap at her desk when the other children napped, and he taught himself how they fit together to make words sitting close to her as she read from children's books and *Life* magazine. The special child thought the tobacco children had the right idea, so he put his head on his desk and slept through the *A*s and the *B*s and the *C*s.

He won't learn, he doesn't learn, he can't learn, the teachers tell the mother. He talks back to his teachers, tries to correct their speech. He was rude to kind Mr. Clary when he came to show the class some magic tricks. You better get him tested. He might be retarded. And he runs funny.

The special child is supposed to be playing at the General Electric Appliance dealer's house with his son David. The son has a tube you blow into and a Mercury capsule shoots up in the air and floats down on a plastic parachute. The special child may have to steal it, but first he decides to go to visit Miss Perk's. Maybe she has a book or something. Miss Perk does not disappoint. She is glad to see the special child. She tells him that the Russians send men up in Mercury-capsule things and don't let them come back down. She says if you tune your radio in just right, you can hear their heartbeats stop. She says if you ever see a red light in the night sky, it's a dead Russian circling the earth forever. *Can I come back and be in your school, Miss Perk?* No, you're too big now. Go home.

Back at the General Electric Appliance dealer's house there's nobody home. It is too far to walk home, so the child lies in the cold grass and watches the grey and orange dusk. At dark, his life will be over. There is a gunshot off in a clay field a ways away, and something like a rocket-fast bumblebee whizzes through the air and thuds into the ground beside the special child. He stays real still. There's not another one. The child is beginning to learn that things can happen to you that would upset the world if you told about them. He doesn't tell anyone about the thing that buzzed and thumped into the ground by his head.

Y'all should do something with that child, people say. The mother takes the child to Cub Scouts. For the talent show, the mother makes a wig out of brown yarn, and the special child memorizes John F. Kennedy's inaugural speech. They laugh at the child in the wig at the show until he begins his speech. Afterward, there's a lecture on drinking water from the back of the toilet after an atom bomb lands on your town, and everybody practices crawling under tables. For weeks afterward, people stop the child and ask him to do the Kennedy thing until finally somebody shoots Kennedy in Texas and the child doesn't have to perform at beer parties and on the sidewalk in front of the grocery store anymore.

The mother starts crying watching the Kennedy funeral on the big TV the father bought to lift her spirits. She doesn't stop. The mother won't get out of bed except to cry while she makes little clothes on her sewing machine. She keeps losing babies, and her mother still won't let her come home. The father sends for the mother's sister. They pack a Thanksgiving lunch and drive to Appomattox to look at the battlefields. It rains and then snows, and they eat turkey and drink wine in the battlefield parking lot. The mother is happy, and the father buys the special child a Confederate hat. After the sister leaves, the mother loses another baby. The father brings the special child another beagle puppy home. The first one, Mud Puddle, ran away in Texas after the father drove it from Lake Charles, Louisiana, to Kirbyville, Texas, strapped to the roof of the car. He had sedated it, he tried to tell people who were nosy along the way. When they got to Texas, there were bugs stuck all in its front teeth like a car grille. When the dog woke completely up, it ran away.

This new dog, in Virginia, the special child calls Hamburger. The mother cries when she sees it in the paper sack. Maybe we need to meet some more friends, the father tells the mother. Okay, the mother says, and wipes her eyes. She always does what her husband tells her to do. She is trying to be a good wife.

There's the big German, Gunther, with the thick accent and

his wife who manage the dairy on the edge of town. They have a German shepherd named Blitz who does whatever Gunther tells it to do. The special child is frightened of the vats of molasses Gunther uses to feed the cows. The child is more interested in the caricatures down in the cellar of Gunther's old house. Gunther's old house was a speakeasy, and someone drew colorful portraits of the clandestine drinkers on the plaster wall behind the bar. They look like people in town, says the special child. It's because the cartoons are the fathers of people in town, says his father.

Gunther's wife finds the special child lying in the cold grass of a pasture watching the sun dissolve in the orange and grey dusk. *You shouldn't do that*, she tells him. If an ant crawls in your ear, it'll build a nest and your brain will be like an ant farm and it'll make you go insane.

Later, Gunther falls into a silage bin, and his body is shredded into pieces the size a cow could chew as cud.

The timber company gives the father a partner so they can reseed the thousands of acres of forests they are clear-cutting down to nothing. Another German. The German knows everything, just ask him, the father says. The German and his wife have two children the special child is supposed to play with. Freddie was the boy's name. Once, when the special child was spending the night, a hurricane came, and Freddie wet the bed and blamed it on the special child. After that, the special child broke a lot of expensive windup cars and trains from the Old Country.

From the helicopter the father uses to reseed the forests farther south, you can still see Sherman's March to the Sea, the old burnage in new-growth trees, the bright cities that have sprung from the towns the drunken Federal troops torched. *Yah, yah, zat iss in der past*, says the German, *you must let it go.*

The father and the German are in North Carolina cutting timber in the bottom of a lake; the dam to make the lake isn't finished yet. The father and the German have become good friends. Sometimes they do their work way back in the deep country away from company supervisors, and sometimes they walk through empty old houses on land their company has bought for timber rights. In the attics they find rare books, old stamps, Confederate money. One day eating lunch in the bottom of the lake, the father and the German figure how much more timber has to be cut before the water will reach the shore. The father then says, *You know, if you were able to figure exactly where the shoreline will be, and buy that land, you could make a small fortune.*

On the weekends, they break their promises to picnic with their families at Indian caves they have found and ride everybody around on the bush motorcycles they use to put out forest fires. Instead, the father and the German spend every extra hour of daylight cutting sight lines with machetes, dragging "borrowed" surveying equipment, and measuring chains around the edge of the empty lake.

The money they give the old black sharecropper for the secret shoreline is all the money they can scrape out of their savings and their banks. The old black sharecropper accepts the first offer the father and the German make on the land left to him by his daddy. Most of the shoreline property they buy from the timber company, but they need an access road through the old black sharecropper's front yard, past his shack. Everyone knows

the lake is coming, but the father and the German don't tell the
black sharecropper the size of their shoreline purchase, just as the
sharecropper doesn't tell them he has also eyeballed where the
shoreline will appear and is going to use their money to build
the state's first black marina with jukeboxes and barbeque pits
right next to their subdivision. He doesn't tell them they just gave
him the seed money to build H. W. Huff's Marina and Playland.

Twenty acres of waterfront property, two points with a long,
clay, slippery cove between them when the dam closes and the
lake floods. The German gets his choice of which half of the
property is his because he was somehow able to put up ten percent more money at the last minute. He chooses the largest point,
the one with sandy beaches all around it. The father gets the wet,
slippery clay bank and muddy point. The father tells the mother
it is time to meet some new friends.

Meet the American Oil dealer, the one with the pretty wife
from Coinjock, North Carolina, a wide grin, and a Big Daddy
next door. Down in the basement of his brand-new brick home
on a brick mantel the oil dealer has a little ship he put together
in college. Most people, if they were even guessing, foot up near
the fire, glass leaning with bourbon, take the little model to be a
Viking ship. It is not a Viking ship even though little fur-tuniced
men seated along both rails pull oars beneath a colorful sail.
Who is that man tied to the mast? asks the special child. Upstairs
the adults play Monopoly in the kitchen and drink beer until
the father drinks a lot of beer and begins to complain about
Sherman's March, and Germans, and it is time to go home.

Later on, the special child is guarding his house with his

Confederate hat and wooden musket while his mother and father are at the hospital having a baby. The oil dealer drives over in his big car and spends the afternoon with the special child. He has a paper sack full of Japanese soldiers you shoot into the air with a slingshot and they parachute into the shrubbery. He shows the special child how to make a throw-down bomb with matchheads and two bolts, but best of all, in a shoe box he has brought the special child the little ship off the brick mantel and tells him who Ulysses was. It is a good story. The only part of the story the child does not quite believe is that somehow Ulysses was older than Jesus. He doesn't say anything to the oil dealer, because the oil dealer was being nice, but he will have to ask Miss Perk about that later.

Here's some pieces that have come off the ship over the years, the oil dealer says. There are a couple of Ulysses' men in his shirt pocket. Thank you, says the child. The child spends the weekend at the oil dealer's house with his wife and children waiting for his mother and father to come home from the hospital empty-handed again.

MORE BAD LUCK. The people at the dam the father calls the idiots keep turning the knobs on the water back and forth. One day the father and the German take their families on a surprise picnic to look at their waterfront property, and way up from their land they can see the lake, way down there over miles of mud. Then one day they come back and find Mr. Huff sitting on the front porch of his sharecropper's shack surrounded by water. *All y'all's land underwater*, says Mr. Huff. *Ain't nothing you can do about it. Man came round and said so. Said it's in your deed.* The father and the German go to see a lawyer. Mr. Huff is right.

One night while his mother is fixing supper, bad luck starts for the special child. He is in the living room, where he had seen an angel pass through Easter morning, watching *The Three Stooges* with the sound turned down real low because *The Three Stooges* upsets his mother. It is a good *Three Stooges*. It was the one where Moe and them run back and forth up and down some train cars and stuff happens and there's a lion loose out of the baggage car, but the best part is when Moe keeps stubbing his toe on somebody's little suitcase every time he runs past it until finally Moe opens the train door and throws the little suitcase off the train into the night. And Moe doesn't stop there; he keeps throwing suitcases off the train, all by himself, he just keeps throwing suitcases off the train in the middle of the night until he looks around and sees that he has thrown everything off the train he possibly could, and then he can relax and be himself again and not be angry anymore. The child has seen this *Three Stooges* before, but this is his favorite. The only problem, this night, watching it with the sound turned down real low while his mother cooks supper waiting for the father to come home, the only problem is that partway through the show, the child hears a truck just outside slam on its brakes and blow its horn, and he hears a dog yelp, and he hears cars slow down and people getting out and men talking and somebody going around the neighborhood knocking on doors and asking whose dog is that, and he hears the people downstairs answer the door, he hears Prince say,

Yeah, he thinks he knows whose dog it is, and he hears Prince call up the staircase to the mother she might want to come down 'cause it looks like a dog looking like their dog got hit by a log truck, and the mother says, *Oh no*, and comes in where the child is watching Moe start to throw the suitcases from the train with the sound turned down real low, and she says, *We'd better go see about Hamburger*, but the child does not move from the TV he is kneeling so close in front of, and the mother has her coat on now and says, *Did you hear me? Hamburger just got hit by a truck*, and still the child does not move, does not make movements to get up, even though he loves his dog and if it were true that his dog were dead, then he would want to die as well, but the child kneels in front of the TV and concentrates on Moe throwing the suitcases off the train, because deep inside him he knows that he can concentrate really hard, like when he learned the Kennedy speech, like when he stepped on a copperhead and the snake would not bite him, even though it should have, the child knows that if he can only concentrate hard enough, Moe will keep throwing everything off the train forever and time will stand still and he will never have to die because he will not have to go downstairs and see his dog twisted and smeared across the street and hear somebody, maybe the nervous log-truck driver, maybe Prince himself, make a joke about what his dog's name used to be and what the dog is now.

He never goes downstairs. He just concentrates in his mind to make the story go on forever, and the news comes on, and his mother comes up from the street, and she looks at him in a new way, like maybe what some people and some teachers say about him is true and maybe they ought to have the special child tested.

The father comes home late that evening after hand-digging a firebreak by almost himself down in some cornpone county where the rednecks came out to watch the fire burn a stand of company pine. For about eighteen hours the father and a pulpwood contractor and his pimply son worked to turn a fire that sometimes stood fifty feet high in the trees over their heads and flanked them a hundred yards either side, sometimes closing. It was good not having to think about his life savings underwater or his sad wife and her lost babies or his strange son or Sherman's March, digging, shoveling, trying to breathe. The father can barely climb the steps up to the top of their house. All he wants is a drink and a hot soak. He has recently started sipping whiskey rather than the beer. His hands are raw, and his back and shoulders ache. In the last hours the fire had lit a turpentine stump and about a hundred snakes had spit themselves up out of the ground and flowed like a stream over his boots. His nerves are still a little jangly.

Up at the top of the stairs stands his special child hardly able to catch his breath from crying so hard and not wanting to wake his mother. The special child clings to his father's pants by the pockets and tells his father he wants to die because his dog Hamburger has, isn't there something his daddy can do about it, and all the father can do about it is pet the boy's head and go back downstairs, get the fire shovel out of his truck, and hope he has enough strength to bury what is left of the little dog in the corner of the cornfield out back of the house.

HERE IS SOME MORE LUCK the German and the father have. One day they are driving the German's Volkswagen bus up a cliff road to check on some land the company is clearing. A log truck loaded with company logs comes around a corner in the middle of the road. The German also always drove in the middle of the road. In the collision the flat-fronted bus folds forward, and the German's legs are pinned and broken in several places. The father is luckier. He raises his arm to his face in time to protect it as he goes through the windshield. In his luck, he goes through the windshield and then over the cliff. He flies over the cliff and lands on some railroad tracks at the bottom. Luckily, the train is late that day. They find his eyeglasses perfectly balanced on a train rail, unbroken.

Here are some of the people who comfort the family: Dr. Jim's wife on the one side of the house. The other next-door neighbors, the Shorts, next to them, the Longs. Down the street a whole block of Misses, Miss Laura, Miss Effie, Miss Roberta, and Miss Henrietta, who used to be a Mrs. until her husband had a heart attack and died the first time they had sex, everyone said. Down the next block, another, older block of spinsters, bitter children of Reconstruction too old to come out to bring food but who send Negro maids with bags of bad fruit from trees in their yards. The barber and his wife come, and the doctor with his third or fourth wife, and Prince and his Italian wife are always there. The father, laid up with a broken leg, busted head, split ribs, and ripped arm, teaches his son to play chess on a little folding set he had from college. The mother sits at the foot of the bed and watches. They all wait for the oil dealer to come. The oil dealer always brings a paper sack of cold beer and ice cream and silly jokes.

You ought to meet my cousin Ruth Ann, the oil dealer tells the mother. She's a lot of fun, and she has a daughter they say ought to be tested too.

※

THE SPECIAL CHILD HAS NEVER SEEN a movie before. He is stunned. *Misty of Chincoteague* on a mile-high drive-in screen. In Ruth Ann's Rambler she drives fast down the middle of the highway, her and the mother in the front seat, the two special children in the backseat. The little girl with impossibly tangled red hair, Christie, says *Misty* is for babies. Christie says if the special child liked *Misty* so much, then he ought to come over and watch the *Invisible Man* on TV on Saturday. She says she knows how to make the house dark even in the afternoon. She says she knows how to make it scary. The special child is still hungover from concentrating on *Misty*. It was almost better than Moe throwing suitcases from the train. While he is thinking this, Christie says to her mother that she is going to vomit. Ruth Ann keeps her Rambler fast down the middle of the highway talking a mile a minute to the mother and says for Christie just to do it out the window. Lean way out and try not to get any on the car.

The special child holds Christie's legs as she leans way out and vomits. It felt as if she would crawl all the way out if he did not hold her. He wraps his arms around her legs and presses his face against her bottom. When she is through, he pulls her in the window, her red hair a solid mass of tangles. The special child helps clean her mouth and face of popcorn and 7Up with an old black slip that for some reason is crumpled up in the floorboard of the backseat of Ruth Ann's rambling car.

WHEN THE FATHER IS FEELING BETTER and up on crutches, he decides to drive them down to Louisiana, and the mother packs that day, even though they will not leave for a week or so. He says they will have a vacation, visit some battlefields on the way down, make a long trip out of it. He will "borrow" a car from the company, a grey sedan with a two-way radio in it.

Before they leave on their vacation, the school invites them to have the special child tested on the first Saturday after school closes for the summer. First grade is over. Bring good pencils.

When the special child shows up with the mother for the testing, the mother is glad to see Ruth Ann there with Christie and Christie's cousin Lynn. They are all three going to be tested together. Most of the test is written and is fun, but some of the test is given by a witch. The witch has cards and blocks and boxes of gears. Once during the testing, Christie has to vomit. Lynn doesn't even care Christie had to vomit. Christie was always vomiting. That is one reason she is being tested.

The closer they get to Louisiana on their vacation, the madder the father gets. Maybe it is all the battlefields. Maybe it is all his broken places in his body. Maybe it is all his land underwater. Maybe it is all the driving time he has to think about everything, driving on the roads before there were interstates between Virginia and Louisiana. Maybe it is going home. Maybe it is because everybody thought he would go real far in life and should be there now, him near the top of his class in chemical engineering at Rice, the people at NASA wanting him bad, and then in his senior year him switching to LSU and forestry so he could be out in the woods by himself all the time. Maybe that is underneath it all, riding in a hot car over asphalt and tar with a trembly wife and special son for days. Maybe he just doesn't like people at all, maybe that is it.

At the mother's mother's house in Louisiana, they have spicy chicken and rice and beer in coolers in the kitchen and black coffee and fried bread and brothers coming in off shifts from the oil fields and refineries to see their big sister, the brothers tossing the special child up in the air and taking him out back to see how they are putting a stock car together. Cousins and uncles and aunts come over, all speaking French, and Uncle Comille with his pigeons and Buddy with his five sons. Only the mother's father sits a little away from things at the table playing solitaire and smoking unfiltered cigarettes. In his life he has been a miner, a baker, a rigger, a cowboy, a pipefitter. To make ends meet, he now drives a mowing tractor at a golf course, bringing home buckets of old golf balls he runs over. Maybe now he is tired.

It is quiet across town at the father's mother's house. You can hear the grandfather clock on the back gallery ticking all through the house. Dinner will always be at high noon. There are no brothers or sisters. One cousin, somewhere. Big Bill, the father's father, lets the special child, his only grandchild, sit in his lap and play with his Shriner's ring and fiddle with his warts. Before high-noon dinner of turkey and dumplings Big Bill balances a shot glass on either arm of his chair, one shot glass filled with bourbon, the other filled with ice water. The special child likes the moments in between the bourbon and the water when the body he is slumped against relaxes and the warm deep breath blown out down on the top of his head smells sweet.

The father's mother is a big woman from Sumrall, Mississippi, who was used to more than her husband has provided over the years. He was away a lot on Huey Long's Special Police force and then later on the railroads, and when he comes home, he goes away on the weekends hunting and fishing with his best friend, Dr. Goldsmith, a Jew. The father's mother did not like Huey Long, and she doesn't like Jews. She had a pet Negro growing up named Scrap. When Big Bill takes their laundry into the black part of town, Big Bill often stays all morning, listening and talking and eating fried-oyster po'boy sandwiches. Now that Big Bill has retired and come home for good, he mostly stays in his shop in the garage putting people's broken clocks together. The big clock at the nearby convent is always stopping, and when he goes over there to fix it, the nuns feed him lunch and make him stay all day.

On a side trip to New Orleans the women go shopping with the father along to watch their bags and Big Bill takes the special child to Jackson Square to feed the pigeons. It is hot, and Big Bill takes the child to some bars off Bourbon Street to get out of the sun and to meet some friends of his from the old days. In the bars are friendly people with parrots on their shoulders, big laughing bartenders in white shirts and black bow ties who give Big Bill his two shot glasses and the child ginger ale colored with maraschino cherry juice. Big Bill lets the child sit on his lap on his bar stool while they watch the street go past the open barroom doors.

Up on a glass shelf in one of the bars they go into, the child sees a windup toy lit from underneath with green and red lights. The bartender takes it down and winds it up and sets it on the bar. A little monkey in a fez plays the drums, nodding his head and kicking his feet. It is like Moe throwing luggage, like Misty swimming in Chincoteague; as long as that monkey keeps playing the drums and nodding his head and kicking his feet, time stands still for the special child. Wind it up again, wind it up. *Can we wind it up again, please, sir?*

Come on, Snort, Big Bill calls his grandson, and Big Bill takes them out of the bar and onto a streetcar out to Audubon Park. A lady in her bathrobe on the streetcar has a plastic flower in her hair and carries a long piece of wrought iron tipped like a spear. It looks like a piece of something she has pulled out of someone's fence. She asks Big Bill for a dime, and he gives her a dollar. Where you going? she asks. I'm taking my grandson to the zoo. Well, say hello to my uncle, says the lady. He works at the zoo? says Big Bill. They got him locked up in the monkey house, says the lady, *'cause he's a monkey's uncle*. Well, we'll say hello, says Big Bill, we're on our way to the monkey house. My boy here seems to like monkeys.

It's incredible, the monkey house. A big castle surrounded by a moat with millions of monkeys playing with themselves like humans and shouting at the tourists and sometimes flinging a handful of poo-poo at the people leaning over the rail.

I want to stay here all day, says the special child. Okay, says Big Bill, we will, and they stay until it is time for them to go.

On their way out, the special child sees a man walking around the monkey house. The man is picking up trash with a nail on the end of a stick. He carries a big burlap sack slung over his shoulder for the stuff he finds. He doesn't even have to bend over to pick it up, because he has the nail on the end of the stick.

Is that that man's job? the special child asks Big Bill.

Yes, says Big Bill, *that's what he does.*

He gets to walk around the monkey house all day with a nail on the end of the stick finding stuff? asks the child.

Yes, says Big Bill.

In the storeroom off the back gallery of Big Bill's house the child finds lots of treasures. There are *National Geographic*s from the very first year. The child mostly likes the castle, ship, and monkey issues. He finds his father's helmet from when his father was in the Army. There is one thing he finds that he likes a lot better than the *National Geographic*s, a box of old photographs of blown-apart people and horses lying dead in snow.

When Big Bill was a young man, he was enlisted from deep within the bayous to fight the Germans in the Great War. Some officers took Big Bill into French towns with them because he spoke a kind of French, and because Big Bill got along well with the French people they met. The French people liked Big Bill and made allowances for the coarser Americans, his Army superiors. As a gift, an officer had given Big Bill a simple box camera. With the simple box camera, Big Bill took photographs of his friends struggling and dying with their horse-drawn artillery in the heavy snows of the Argonne forest. The only happy photograph was taken by a stranger on the returning troopship—a very thin Big Bill and two other soldiers, all who were left of the cannonade they had been.

When the special child pulls the box of photographs out and

asks about it, they take it away from him, and on his later visits the box is gone.

Here is something you can play with, the grandmother tells the special child. She sets an old Royal typewriter on the dining room table. *Write me a letter, write me a story.* The child tries to type the story of Misty of Chincoteague in several sentences. It takes most of the afternoon.

When it is time to go back to Virginia, they spend one last night at the mother's old house, and she cries and begs to stay. Here, take some food I am making for you for the trip, the mother's mother says, ignoring her crying. The mother's mother cooks spicy food and fries up some bread, and this makes the father angry because he hates when his clothes smell like fried bread. The child is afraid he will have to return to Virginia with his father by himself.

They have a big going-away barbeque for the mother, and her brothers tie her up in the backyard and wash her hair for her with the hose until she says uncle. Everybody laughs except the father, who watches from the garage where the stock car and tools are, sipping beer. When the child tries to save his mother, one of his uncles sets him on top of the garage roof and later makes him ride a pony.

Sometimes on the drive back to Virginia, because the company grey sedan with the two-way radio looks like an unmarked police car, the father drives up behind people he thinks are driving too fast and flashes his lights and makes them pull over, then he speeds off. He stops doing this when in Georgia he accidentally pulls over an unmarked police car and the state trooper is very angry at the father. Later on in North Carolina, the father seethes and speeds faster.

It has been so hot while they have been away in Louisiana that the candles the mother had stuck in the Chianti bottles are drooped over on the mantel.

There is a lot of mail. There is a letter from the invention company where the father has sent them an invention. It is for a device that hooks onto a kite string that sends paper airplanes up to the kite and then releases the airplanes so they can float to the ground. The father had gotten the idea watching the special child trying to slingshot his Japanese parachutists as high as he can in the backyard. The father tried to explain the idea to his brothers-in-law in Louisiana, and they were polite about it, but you could tell they didn't understand why anyone would want an invention like that. Right on the spot, the brothers-in-law took some pipes and welded together a cannon that shot old golf balls about a hundred yards. You can take it back to Virginia with you, they told the child when they were leaving, giving him the cannon, and they said good luck to the father about his invention, even if they didn't understand it. When the family got home from Louisiana, the invention company didn't understand the invention and they didn't want it, either.

In the mail are test results. One test result says the mother is most likely pregnant again. The other test result says the special child is eligible for a special school if the father can afford it.

The father goes down to check on his underwater property. While he and his family have been away in Louisiana, the idiots at the dam finally adjusted the water levels on the lake just right.

The shoreline is exactly where he and the German had predicted it would be. In the lowering fluctuations of the lake all the German's beautiful sand has washed along the father's shoreline and blanketed his property with long, broad beaches. Where the German's beautiful beaches had been are ugly slick stretches of slippery red clay corrupted through and through by the black roots of drowned trees. *Zat iss in der past, you must let it go*, the father tells the angry German. The German and his family move away.

In the fall the special child starts second grade. His second-grade teacher is Miss Caroon. Miss Caroon has seen his test results, so she lets him spend as much time as he wants reading *The Boxcar Children* and Mark Twain in the cloakroom while the other children struggle with Dick and Jane and Baby Sally and Spot. Miss Caroon lets him wear his father's Army helmet in the classroom if he wants to, and she lets him try to pass off the wad of Confederate money he always carries. At Thanksgiving, when he draws the Pilgrims coming to the New World in a Chinese junk greeted by Indians selling Live Bait and Cold Beer, she hangs his picture on the wall with all the rest without extraordinary comment.

Miss Caroon gives the children in her class a list of words from which to make a story. In the stories the class turns in, dogs get up on the furniture when they aren't supposed to or someone finds a coin. From the special child she receives "The Ancient Castle," in which a Good King goes away to conquer an enemy and while he is gone an Evil King comes and lays siege to the Good King's castle. The Evil King's men scale the walls, and some of the Good King's favorite men are shot full of arrows and beheaded. Just when all seems to be lost, everyone looks up and sees a brilliant flash of light on a distant hill. It is the sun shining off the Good King's shield. The Good King and his men come and slaughter the Evil King and all the Evil King's men. The people in the Good King's castle are so happy, they have a huge banquet and feast on roast duck and turkey. After they have eaten all they can eat, they begin singing the Good King's favorite songs. Miss Caroon reads the child's story out loud to the class. She especially likes the last sentence in the story and takes her time sounding it out—*And the singing went on for days.*

Miss Caroon hands back the stories, and the child receives an A-minus because he misspells "Ancient" in the title. This is a very good story, she tells the child. When his mother comes to visit on Parents' Day, Miss Caroon tells her that her son is a special child, that he could be a writer someday if he wanted to be one. The mother shakes her head sadly and tells Miss Caroon the truth. She has to tell Miss Caroon that all the child wants to be when he grows up is the man who walks around the monkey house all day with a nail on the end of a stick.

⁂

SAY YOU ARE THE SPECIAL CHILD. Say one reason you are special is because there is something wrong with your legs. You cannot run. Your legs will not move fast enough. When you try to run, your hips click and pop. When you have to run a race, like at the going-away party at a doctor's house in the old town, when everyone was running toward the doctor's house that would burn completely to the ground the next year, you pretend to trip and fall and not finish the race. You avoid footraces; you avoid running at all. When something bad happens and everyone else runs away, rocks thrown through greenhouse glass, loose spikes thrown at passing caboose windows, fishing boats untethered along a riverbank, you know you will have to face whoever is coming at you in their anger. You learn you must never get caught.

In the new town the teachers don't say you are special as the teachers did in the old town. They use the word "slow." And you are slow. But they also say you are slow when you are sitting at your desk unable to color the state bird. You can't get the red crayon to work on the cardinal in a way that makes the teacher happy. Your father has said to be careful about signing your name to anything, so you don't put your name on your homework. A suspicious teacher has said that if your parents are really from Louisiana, you must be able to speak French. *Oui*, you say. You try to speak with a French accent, you still try to spend your Confederate money, you still wear your father's Army helmet to school. No one can understand what you are saying, and big boys from out in the county want to fight you in line to the cafeteria. They come up behind you and flip off your helmet and you have to fight them almost every day. The fighting finally stops when you break a boy's hand. When your mother finds out, she cries because she is afraid the boy is the son of a new friend of hers. You get the feeling it was selfish of you to break the boy's hand.

A good afternoon in the new town is when the school is struck twice by lightning. Everyone else starts crying when the lightning strikes the swing set first. You stand at the window. It's raining and thundering and the lightning strikes the roof, but the sun is also shining, and you heard from your father's mother that when it rains and the sun is shining, it means the Devil is beating his wife. As the big boys from the county and all the little girls cry for their mommies and the teacher is shouting for everyone to get into the cloakroom, you clap and laugh and shout, *The Devil is beating his wife! The Devil is beating his wife!* The children and teacher are afraid of your loud laughter, you can tell by their looks as they crowd into the cloakroom as you stand by the open window getting soaked by the windblown rain, the special child.

One morning you do not have to go to school. Your father does not put on his forest clothes—khaki shirt, denim jeans, snake pistol, long-sheath knife, the boots with wire laces that won't burn in case he gets caught in a forest fire and has to make a run for it. He puts on a coat and a tie, and you get in the car with him. He drives you to Richmond, through swamps, low woodlands, fields turned over for peanuts and corn. Neither of you speaks, there's just the tires on the corduroy road and his flying-tiger class ring clicking the window when he lifts his cigarette ash to the rolled-down crack at the top. You always keep an eye out for the tiger, you never know when it may fly across your face.

Your father turns the grey sedan in to a long driveway between green lawns to a place that looks like a museum. Your father signs you in, and you take an elevator upstairs. The place smells like linoleum wax and medicine and shitty diapers.

You and your father sit on folding chairs in a long dark hallway with other fathers and mothers and what an odd boy who lives in the place later calls *sin spawn*: children with withered legs, legs of different lengths, bent-up legs, legs in steel and leather braces, hobbling kids crying and carrying the smell of places where people live who tote water in buckets from a well and go to the bathroom in sheds out back. A lot of the people waiting have long greasy hair that needs cutting. You can tell some are missing teeth when they talk and smoke and spit in the metal trash can by the exam room door.

A woman in a white uniform comes out with a clipboard and hands it to your father. You can read the top of the paper, and you understand why you are special when you read CRIPPLED CHILDREN'S HOSPITAL.

The doctor has seen your X-rays. He twists your legs and makes your hips crack and pop on the white-papered table. The doctor doesn't answer your father's questions. The doctor says he will try nails in your hips. Your father wants to know if the doctor will put the nails in your hips himself. The doctor doesn't answer your father. He says nails are the best remedy. Your father asks if there is any other *remedy*, and he says it in a way that makes him sound like a smart-ass. The doctor stares at your father and says loudly, *With or without the nails, your son will probably be in a wheelchair by the time he's thirty anyway.*

To cheer you up, your father takes you to the Hollywood Cemetery, where some of your heroes are buried, President Jefferson Davis, Major Generals J. E. B. Stuart and George Pickett. You and your friends have spent many afternoons playing Pickett's Charge in the park across from the Episcopal church, running into withering cannon and musket fire, and because of your legs you are always the first casualty as the minié balls rip into your arms and throat, falling dying in the grass, sometimes

crawling beneath the azalea bushes where Robert E. Lee sits
astride his iron-grey horse Traveller, him saying down to you
sadly, *I'm sorry, I'm sorry, it was all my fault.*

After you visit the grave of the doctor who amputated Stonewall Jackson's arm and tended to Lee's heart attack on the eve of
Gettysburg, you go see the big black iron dog that guards a little
girl's grave. By the time you get to the grave of Jefferson Davis's
five-year-old son, Joe Davis, you are ready to go home.

AT THE HOSPITAL THEY strip you naked and scrub you with
tar-smelling delousing soap in a deep sink in an old tiled room
full of drains even though you had a bath that morning before
leaving home with your family. A nurse takes the green cardboard
suitcase your mother had packed for you that morning and says
she'll deliver it to your father in the reception office. It's the green
cardboard suitcase you used to carry your cat in. Here are your
new clothes, nice and clean, with somebody else's name in the
worn waistband of the donated shorts and in the collars of the two
old summer camp shirts. One of the shirts is a good one, yellow,
red, and white madras, and in the coming months you will trade
for it back when it goes through the laundry and is given to someone else.

Here is the T-shirt to sleep in, here is a fresh sheet for your
bed, once a week put the top sheet on the bottom, the fresh sheet
on top, and here is your bed on the sunporch. The boys' ward
is crowded in summer. Your bed looks out over the rigging and
masts, the bars and chains of the playground swing sets. That

night it will all look like shipwrecks in the grey streetlight when you turn away from the crying around you and stare out through the metal safety rails of your bed.

Your mother sat in your father's car in the parking lot earlier that afternoon nursing your baby sister because your mother's luck has changed. She's had a baby and she's going to hell. She and another lady went into the little Catholic church to put fresh flowers on the altar one Saturday afternoon, and the priest came out of the sacristy with a rope belt and Scotch on his breath. Women in culottes defiling the altar. *Whores!* The priest swung the rope belt, and in her weekly call to her own mother later in Louisiana, your mother says she has left the Church for good.

Then you are going to hell, her mother tells her. *Goodbye.* On the extension, you hear someone take a breath quickly after your grandmother says this, and don't know if it's your mother or the long-distance operator who sometimes listens in and lives down your street in a sorrow-filled house with her three children who used to be four children until one drowned in the frozen pond behind the cemetery like a lot of people seem to do, including Mrs. Richardson one street over.

From your sunporch bed that afternoon you saw your father return to the car with your green suitcase and tell your mother something, and it seemed she didn't understand, but later you could tell she was crying as she nursed your little sister.

Your father walks over to the empty playground where no one is allowed because it is not playtime and he sits in one of the swings and you watch him chain-smoke for a while until he sees your mother burping your sister and he looks at his watch. A nervous boy comes up to you and says some kid died that morning. You figure out you got the dead kid's bed. When you look out next, your father is gone, there's an empty swing swinging in the swing set. In the morning you go out on the playground with all the other crippled children and you find the swing where your father sat, the smoked tobacco and cigarette butts ground into the ashy dust.

IN THE NEXT DAYS they draw your blood and take your temperature. They X-ray you some more and forget you in a hallway until suppertime. They make you walk naked in front of an auditorium of young student doctors and nurses from a college. *Walk. Run. Stop. Stand on one leg. Hop. Run some more.* Also in the audience are boys your age and girls your age. They see how you can't run naked, how you can't hop naked, how you can barely walk naked. They laugh at first until they realize in a few minutes a nurse will remove their gowns and make them jump, run, walk, and hobble naked, too.

One day after lunch, instead of a nap, a nurse takes you and her purse out in front of the hospital to wait for a taxicab. The taxicab takes the two of you to a laboratory downtown. By the way the nurse pets your head, you know this is going to be bad. They give you a shot that makes you drowsy and begin to dream, but you don't fall all the way asleep. While you are drowsy and beginning to dream, they lay you on your side and push long needles into your spine. Somebody in your dream is screaming.

It's you.

Later in the taxicab back to the hospital the nurse holds you in her arms like a backseat pietà, the sunlight burns your eyes, and the telephone wires hang and loop, hang and loop. In the hospital auditorium you had noticed these words painted in large letters over the stage: SUFFER THE LITTLE CHILDREN TO COME UNTO ME.

Who said that? you ask the nurse who took you to the laboratory, the nurse who sometimes sneaks Coke in your metal spout cup when everybody else gets tap water. Nurse Wilfong.

Jesus. Jesus Christ, she says.

What kind of jerk would want little children to suffer? you wonder.

Nurse Wilfong says you're constipated. They keep track of everyone's bowel movements in a ledger. You didn't know you had to report a bowel movement while you were still walking around, if they hadn't sent you upstairs yet to let the young student doctors practice taking you apart and nailing you back together.

Nurse Wilfong wants you to drink chalky stool softener while you want to talk about what a jerk Jesus must be if that's what He said about children and suffering. It's creepy, like the older boys going around saying a kid down in North Carolina went into a department store bathroom and some man cut his penis off with a pocketknife. The older boys say it was in the newspaper.

The hospital is crowded with children from Appalachia with knees that have to be cut up and legs that have to be sawed off. They're a pretty happy bunch. They love the food so much you give them yours, you don't eat it anyway. The first night you went into the lunch-table room there was a black kid sneezing snot into his plate of food right before the blessing. The woman who ran the lunch table made everyone slide down one plate so you could squeeze in, and you got the plate with the droplets of snot on the rim, the rest of the snot having disappeared into the stewed tomatoes and cabbage and boiled meat. The Appalachian kids start eating off your plate as soon as it's set down in front of you. One of the Appalachian kids had been sent home with a long cast on his leg, and when he comes back and they cut off the cast, they find bugs have nested in there.

The black kid who blew snot all over your food is on a respirator now. You lie awake and watch the stoplight change out on Brook Road and wonder if there was enough of something in that one spoonful of stewed tomatoes you choked down so that you'll start coughing up bloody snot yourself. The ward overflows with deformity and crying kids at night. It's been two weeks, maybe they've forgotten about you again.

Then one night they get you.

The night nurse and the night porter jerk and wheel your bed into the prison spotlight of the night nurse's desk lamp so she can better see to tie No Breakfast signs to your bed rails. The young doctors will be waiting upstairs for you in the morning. They'll make Ben or Howard or one of the other black orderlies come down and fetch you. You hope you will come back alive because everyone knows, even the little boys on the other end of the ward, that not everybody comes back from upstairs. Sometimes boys end up on a gurney covered in bloody sheets and tossed-off scrubs down in the basement waiting for a station wagon from the state to fetch you, Big Mike says. Big Mike has burns over ninety percent of his body and carries a single condom in an otherwise empty wallet. He knows things. You begin to pray to God directly, forget the creepy men's room Christ who wants you to suffer, and you hope somebody has called your parents because sometimes they forget to do that too.

NO ONE TELLS YOU that you will wake up in a body cast, so it is a surprise when you wake up and you are in a cast that reaches from under your arms and goes down to your knee on one side and down to your toes on the other. You vomit a lot coming out of the anesthesia as harelip kids bang around under your bed playing cowboys. You remember trying to push yourself out of the cast like an insect molting its shell and only the searing burn of the stretching of fresh stitchery covering the hammered-in nails around one hip makes you stop.

The heat of the place in the day and the fear of roaches that might crawl down into your cast at night make it hard to sleep. The nurses put you out on the smaller sunporch that has some books that aren't worth reading, mostly schoolbooks written before World War II. For a while, there are two Jerrys. One Jerry is the guy who is called the Human Skeleton. His clothes look like scarecrow rags. He ranges around on his bed waiting for someone to come too close so he can bite the person with his large buckteeth. He has one large testicle that sways back and forth when he crouches at the foot of his bed, chomping at the air. Later, when you are in a wheelchair and you can sit beside his bed and feed him crayons, he lets you pet his head like a dog and he pats your arm and howls.

The other Jerry is from Appalachia. He has calm, even features and a trusting smile and the eyes of a schoolbook pioneer standing on a mountaintop leading a wagon train into a lush green valley beyond. Already the doctors have taken off one of his legs. In the daytime it doesn't seem to bother him too much. But at night, as you watch for roaches crawling along your bed rail so you can flick them off, you see Jerry in silhouette against the Brook Road streetlight, and you see him stare down at the place where his leg used to be. You pretend you are asleep. Jerry throws himself back onto his pillow and Jerry cries, and you know he is trying not to. You want to tell him that it's all right, that everyone here cries at night.

Here is a miracle—you find a game board and a box of chess pieces, none missing. You teach Jerry to play chess. At nap time, when all must be quiet, Jerry sets up the board on a small table beside his bed. He touches each of your pieces with just the tip of a finger, waiting to see if that is the piece you want to move. You nod your head. He moves the piece. You clear your throat for the number of spaces, point a finger to adjust direction.

When Jerry moves his pieces, you see he's playing a cautious defensive game. Castling confounds him. Only when he almost makes the most fatal errors do you snap your fingers and he looks up to see you tapping your temple, telling him, *Think!* You don't want to keep beating him, and he knows this and tries harder. Just when you are about to quit one afternoon, he puts you in check, and if he weren't missing a leg and you weren't flat on your back in a body cast, you'd both get up and shake hearty hands. Instead, the two of you clap without making a sound because it is nap time and all must be quiet.

ON SUNDAY MORNINGS, Jerry's family comes down from the mountains somewhere near Cumberland Gap. They leave their houses in the dark and drive across the state just to be with Jerry for a few hours. They stand there and hold on to his clothes as if he might float away. Jerry's family doesn't bring him anything to eat, and you know it is because they don't have anything to bring. His parents look at Jerry in his face and hold on to his clothes and Jerry looks down at the leg that he has left, and there you are across the way, with grease all over your fingers, eating a fried chicken box lunch your parents have brought, knowing Jerry's family is all hungry and will drive back across the state without stopping. Your mother has also brought you a toy with the fried chicken box lunch, a blue plastic plate and a stick. The idea is to spin the plate on the end of the stick. The first time you try to spin the blue plastic plate on the end of the stick it flies off and hits Jerry's father on the back. Jerry's father picks up the blue plastic plate and kindly passes it back to your mother, and she smiles and hands it to you and you are ashamed.

Sundays bring the young seminarians, the practice preachers, murmuring down the hallway, doing God's work, visiting the sick in their Hush Puppies shoes. All smiles until they smell you. They can't control you around the piano wheeled out of a classroom, can't make you love Jesus, fail to threaten you with the prophet Elisha, who called down she-bears to rip the forty-two little mocking children to shreds, you all laughing at the violent story with spitting harelips and cleft palates and brandishing canes and crutches, nudging the seminarians into the clutches of the Human Skeleton and brain-damaged Dennis, who'll bite and strangle them, the practice preachers looking, as all visitors ultimately do, for a nurse and a quick exit.

But the men from the barber college who come to cut your hair! Clicking down the hall in polished loafers, laughing and goofing, their smiles steadfast as they round the corner and smell you, see you, mangy mongrels with overgrown bowl cuts from the hills, crew cuts from the piedmont gone to seed post-surgery, matted twists of bed-headed hair pressed against pillows twenty-four hours a day. The barbers come whistling with jokes and songs and gum, and they touch you, cradle your heads in their hands as they trim, hold you in their arms so you can safely lean over the edge of the bed in your body casts as they open your faces with their scissors, telling each crippled child who he looks like from movies and men's magazines, the barbers clipping and snipping at the dirty ropes of hair falling off the beds onto the floor for Ben the porter to sweep up.

The men from the barber college sweep the beds with little brooms from the deep pockets of their white jackets, which you all keep peering into for more gum, and there is always more gum! And from the deep pockets they pull the pint flasks of cologne and cooling colored water they clap on their hands and rub around your necks and on your faces and through your hair like a blessed baptism that opens your lungs for the first time in forever with its fragrance, remembering you to a world beyond that doesn't smell like bedpans, pissed pants, dirty sheets, the deathly perfume stench of yourselves rotting in rancid plaster.

Everyone wishes the barbers came every week like the practice preachers but the barbers do not. The only good thing the practice preachers bring is the pornography, the vivid picture books of martyrs led and bound to rocks where they have their hands chopped off by laughing scoundrels. All the boys like the pictures so much the practice preachers stop bringing them. The practice preachers can't stand how you all laugh at the guys with the chopped-off hands, the way they sit with their faces turned up toward the clouds, blood gushing from their bloody stumps like broken red pipes, their hangdog tongues, their mangy shoulder-length hair, their eyes staring stupidly into heaven.

YOUR FATHER IS COMING for you in a station wagon, the head nurse says. You say goodbye to Nurse Wilfong, who bathes you every day, you say goodbye to Big Mike, the boy with the melted face, and give him your transistor radio. You give your best friend, Michael Christian, the black boy in perpetual leg braces, all of your contraband—an old Christmas tin of stale pretzels and the rubber-band slingshot metal-tipped balsa jets some Shriners had handed out and were confiscated after everyone shot them stuck into the acoustic tile ceiling. You give the Human Skeleton a tin metal truck and the little daredevil figure that shot out of the Cracker Jack box prize cannon. He breaks it the first time he fires it. You write a note to the girl on the girls' ward you talked to on the lawn when Hogan's Heroes came, Colonel Klink telling you he had a son named Mark. You tell the girl you're sorry, it's over, you're going home. The young nurse who had passed all the notes back and forth reads it and laughs and throws it away.

You say goodbye to Ben the porter, who always gave you a pony blanket at nap time that didn't smell like diarrhea and who always saved you a little paper cup of pineapple juice when nap time was over. You say goodbye to Jerry, who now doesn't have any legs at all.

Two hours home, everything recedes through the back station wagon window, you in your body cast on a pallet of old blankets—Richmond, the cigarette factories, the signs to the Crater, then the plank road, the fields of peanut stacks, and the dark alleys of swamp road. A man from your father's work, a man who survived Omaha Beach when ninety-eight percent of his company did not, who loses his only son to a tiny complication in a minor surgery, helps your father lift you from the back of the station wagon. The man from your father's work carries you like a piece of precious furniture he is afraid to break, into your house, tilting you at the door because your plastered legs are cast too wide, and you momentarily grasp the old brass door knocker etched with the name of the family who had lived there long before your family, Livesay.

Your father has rented a hospital bed and pushed it against the window of a downstairs bedroom no one sleeps in. It is Indian summer and still hot and your house does not have air-conditioning. The cotton in your cast is hot and your legs itch and you wonder if the little things you feel down in the plaster that you can't reach with an unbent coat hanger are trickling sweat or something nesting like the things they found in the kid from Appalachia's cast when they cut it off. You know you smell bad, and sometimes your mother walks through waving a cloud of disinfectant spray in the air, looking at the ceiling as if that is where the smell is coming from and not from you.

You don't want visitors and your best friend, David, understands this and he and his dog Wolf come and talk to you through the window screen. David is The Preacher down the street's third son of four, you'd been warned away from him by the lady next door the day you moved in. He's trouble, the lady'd said. She said you ought to just play with her son Jim. When redheaded David came around your backyard that first afternoon to steal your moving crates and boxes, you became best friends to this day, fifty years running. Sometimes Wolf, the large blue collie, sleeps in the shrubbery under your window, you can hear his tags clink in the evenings as he settles in, he's a good dog. The clinking of his tags always calms you. He had slept there many nights the two summers before when David came over and you two played a Monopoly game that you made last from Memorial Day until Labor Day, sheaves of wide-ruled paper documenting the moves of phantom players, the building of triple hotels, and alternating ownership of the bank.

Your mother has your baby sister to tend to and she has you. You have to teach your mother how to bathe you, how to empty a bedpan, when to bring a urinal, how to help you flip over so she can change your sheets. Your father doesn't come into your room much. No one is happy except your baby sister when they lift her into the playpen of your hospital bed and she crawls all over you and sits beside your head and laughs while she slaps your face and you let her.

There are two positions in the body cast, faceup and facedown. From either position you can watch your street go by. There is Augie who lives in the maid's house across the street. He gets up at dawn to drive by the cemetery to check the lights on the radio tower before driving to the little studio in the low-end strip mall on the river to warm up the transmitter. In those days he is the voice of the town, and everyone listens to his morning show—the news, the weather, the twenty-year-old songs, the birthdays and anniversaries, the lost and found, the church supper announcements. *Be Still and Know*, the inspirational program with the church organ lead-in, the sports scores, the gentle chiding of the town elders when they needed it, the dedications of songs when someone needed it, the remembrances of the people who needed remembering, and the marathon fund-raising in the window of the Chevrolet dealership owned by the man whose wife taught Sunday school and was a member of the Hitler Youth, the fund-raising for the star football player who'd fallen from a tree retrieving a shot squirrel and broke his back.

There is the lady walking past who works at the phone company, petite, same sweater, even in summer, purse held tightly almost to her throat, her shoulders lift as she walks as if she is always cold and shivering. Every Sunday night your parents call your mother's parents down in Louisiana. To make a long-distance call, you have to dial zero and ask an operator for help. There are only a handful of operators, and you recognize their voices, like this lady in the sweater from down the street who lives in the falling-down house next to the Christian church with her four children, an older daughter who is a high school cheerleader, two twin boys who were sometimes left at their grandparents' house while the mother worked the switchboard, and a little girl. Last winter when the pond where Mrs. Richardson drowned herself froze over, the two twin boys and a friend of theirs from down on the other end of the street took a kickball out on the ice, and they fell through. One of the twins managed to crawl ashore and get help, but by the time everybody got there, there was only the hole in the ice where the two boys disappeared. Nearby, the kickball sat on the ice in the melting sun. They pulled the bodies out, but nobody wanted to go out any farther on the thinning ice to get the kickball. The next day the grandfather went down there with a shotgun and blew the kickball apart, shooting it again and again until it disappeared. Both families moved away, and the church, which owned the falling-down house, tore it down and made it into the parking lot that it is to this day.

Once, listening in on the extension phone when your parents call Louisiana and the operator is the lady who has lost her child, you can hear the sad story in her voice even when she only says *You are connected*, and then your grandfather answers the phone *Allô?* and your mother says *Comme c'est va, cha?* and your grandfather, who misses your mother, who is his eldest daughter who is so far away and who has lost her faith, you can hear in his low voice that he will not be putting your grandmother on the line as he says *Pas mal, not bad, chérie, not bad. Et tu?* And then you faintly hear someone crying on the line somewhere, and you don't know if it is your mother knowing her mother has not forgiven her or if it is the lady from down the street listening in, her operator's mouthpiece in a tight little first clenched against her sweatered shivering breast.

There's the blind man passing, the man who reupholsters furniture by touch, he comes tapping with his white and red cane, red-lidded, rolled-back eyes, a half smile, and even if you hold your breath, he turns his head and looks into your window, neatly raising his right foot to miss the place where the walnut tree has levered up the sidewalk to trip him in front of your house.

There goes one of the sisters who used to babysit you, the sisters sharing a bedroom in a house in the next block where one night a hand holding a screwdriver floated into their room through the punctured window screen between their beds. When the older sister used to babysit you, she used to draw moody pencil sketches of old rowboats rotting on chains in a cypress swamp.

There's David's father, The Preacher, getting into their ancient blue station wagon, pipe bitten down, himself nearly blind in one eye, a large enough man so you can hear him humming a hymn from two doors down and across the street. *Lord, plant my feet on higher ground.* You miss the parsonage where you spent as much time as you did in your own house before your hips happened, a place that always smelled like bacon and coffee, the old pages and leather of books about God and the Apostles, Virginia history, and places in the world where The Preacher intended to travel. The Preacher and his wife, Janet, are like your other parents, you being the fifth brother to the four sons they already have. The Preacher never holds it against any of you for being boys prone to mischief. Sometimes at The Preacher's church the carillon goes off unexpectedly during the day, sometimes broadcasting "Chopsticks," "Shave and a Haircut," or the four-note opening of the *Twilight Zone* theme. Once one of his elder sons rummaged through his war loot and hung a three-story Nazi banner from the attic window on Flag Day, sending Mrs. Butler, the school music teacher, into a telephone pole when she saw it, you and David goose-stepping on the front sidewalk as an elder son Sieg Heiled from the attic window. And later, when you and David pin some children down in a garage, shooting them in their butts with David's new BB gun, The Preacher comes home to where you and David are sitting on the porch and quietly asks to see the new rifle that he calmly wraps around a tree in the yard before going in to dinner. The Preacher says he did not believe in the concept of Original Sin until he had children.

The Saturday afternoon your father covers your window with thick grey plastic Mr. Panton two doors down is cutting his grass with the town's only electric lawn mower. It is late fall and the rye-grass is lush and the sun is leaving early. Your house is cold and drafty, and your father is stapling plastic on the window frames. He is a black shadow on the plastic outside your window and you're glad you're not having to hold the ladder so he can climb to the second-story windows because you never hold the ladder just right. Once, when he almost fell, you'd let go so he wouldn't land on top of you. Mr. Panton's eyesight is poor and he has run over the cord to his electric lawn mower so many times that the cord is forever shortened in electrical tape splicings. He can't reach the far corners of his yard anymore. You hear Mr. Panton run over his cord again in the dusk. Your father's shadow moves off and your grey window to the world fades to black.

The next morning will be Sunday, and your father will load you into the back of the station wagon and take you back to Richmond.

꙳

WHEN THEY CUT YOU OUT of your cast, you are surprised there are no bugs inside, but your legs have atrophied into two long hairy sticks of rotting flesh. You can scrape hair and dead skin off the bone with your fingernail. Later you hear that doctors think leaving children in body casts for a long time is not a good idea.

They wheel you down to the ward, and it's been cleft palate season. There are a lot of children running around with complicated black stitchery on their upper lips. Some look like little Hitlers, others look like black-whiskered cats. They put you on the big sunporch with some older black boys, and you're glad to find Michael Christian. Nurse Wilfong comes to see you and says how you've grown, must have been your mama's cooking, and you look toward the little sunporch and ask where Jerry is, and she holds your face in her hands and bends over and says, *Jerry died.*

Out on the big sunporch it's cold at night. The older black boys are all from Richmond. There's Dennis in the corner bed. He keeps saying, *I used to be smart but then I got a brain tumor and now I'm stupid.* The little boys tease him and if they get too close he'll strike at them with palsied arms and try to strangle them. Michael Christian inherited your old transistor radio from Big Mike when Big Mike left but the nurses have taken it away from him. There's a black boy named Columbus Floyd who looks like an old man already bent over a cane waiting to be taken upstairs. You nickname him Chris and he likes it. He doesn't want to learn how to play chess, but he'll play checkers with you for hours and you never win a single game. He keeps the little boys away from Dennis's bed, they're afraid of his cane.

They take you to physical therapy to teach you to walk again. There are no muscles left in your legs, and if it weren't for Charles, the black PT assistant, holding you up with a belt looped under your arms, you would fall more than you do. There's a new physical therapist who takes your extended atrophied leg over the edge of a padded table and then pushes it down so hard he tears something in your leg and you scream and pound on his back with your fists until Charles comes over and says, *What the hell you doing, man?* The new guy doesn't work there much longer.

The woman who replaces him performs a miracle on a boy from Appalachia. The boy has never walked a step in his life. He lives in his wheelchair and is old enough to masturbate furiously all the time under a blanket, then he asks a nurse to clean him up. He only sleeps in his wheelchair; when they put him in bed, he's frozen in the wheelchair position and says all night out loud, keeping everyone awake, *My legs are tighter than a cork in a bottle, my legs are tighter than a cork in a bottle.* So the night nurse and Ben have to lift him down into his wheelchair, where he masturbates himself to sleep.

The new physical therapist and Charles soak the boy in a stainless steel vat of hot water and massage his legs and back for hours. Charles gets the boy up on crutches and he is surprisingly tall. He has a way of talking that sounds like a female cat yowling when she is mounted by a tom and the tom has his teeth in her neck. Everyone is a little frightened of the boy now that he is on crutches. He follows people a little too closely like he would like to kick their crutches out from under them. When he can finally walk just using a cane, a woman and two men from Appalachia come to get him. If they are related to him or to each other, it is hard to see. They feel like the people who once tried to get David into a car with North Carolina license plates the Saturday afternoon you were in a part of town you were not supposed to be in, which is why you never told your parents. These people from Appalachia come to fetch the tall boy with an old beat-up wheelchair that he happily sits in when he sees it. When the nurses say he can walk now, he doesn't need the wheelchair, it's a miracle, the people mock the nurses and run out of the place pushing the boy laughing ahead of them. One of the men looks back, and his look dares anyone to follow.

By Christmastime, all the black boys on the big sunporch have been cut up and nailed back together. When their families come to visit, it is like a party. Often they come from church in their church clothes, and they have real fried chicken and they always make you a plate. Sometimes their preachers come with them, and their preachers pray over the boys and they'll pray over you if they catch you looking and you're always looking, so they pray over you, too.

Your parents haven't been coming, because you are supposed to go home soon. The wards are emptying out for the holidays, and there are just a few of you left. The doctors fix Big Mike's face and Big Mike runs away. The police come and walk with Ben around the playground in the dark shining their flashlights. The night nurse tells you Big Mike didn't run away home, she called, they don't expect him to show up there. Big Mike has a brother in the Navy, so maybe he'll turn up in Norfolk.

The society people and the charity people and the practice preachers come and go with their old donated toys and oranges and little broken candy canes, and you're happy not to be bothered anymore. You worry about Michael Christian. You realize no one has ever come to see him on Sundays, and when the other black families come, he is always on the edge of his bed leaning in to them, the first to laugh too loud at their jokes, trying to butt into their conversations. He wears shorts even in winter because he never goes outside, there is always some sort of metal brace on his legs. You watch him over there in his bed, in his shorts, taking the batteries out of his precious transistor radio and putting them back in. You see all the years of scars up and down his legs and you begin to realize that Michael Christian will never go home, that this is his home, he lives at Crippled Children's Hospital.

The day your father is supposed to come get you he doesn't show up. Two days go by. When he does show up, you are angry. He wants to know if you would like a pastrami sandwich. *Okay*, you say.

There is traffic getting out of the car. You are almost hit by a truck crossing the street to catch up with your father. The sidewalk in front of the delicatessen is broken. Your father is not like Charles. Your father drinks beer and talks to the waitress. You say nothing. On the way out he buys some pickled herring for your mother and a halvah bar for you.

At home the Christmas tree is up, your mother cooks shrimp Creole for you. She comes into the bathroom one night because you have been sitting in the bathtub so long staring down at your hairy skeletal legs in the cold water. She wants to know what you want for Christmas. You tell her you'd like a saw to cut off your goddamned legs.

There's a Christmas sing one night around the old magnolia tree in the park and your father wants you all to go. It has been snowing, and there is ice everywhere. You really don't want to go out on the ice on crutches. Your father has been drinking bourbon and says it will be good for you to get out and get some air and see some people. You really don't want to go. *You're going, goddamn it*, your father says. You make it out to the car without falling on the ice on your crutches but you slip a couple of times, it's dark. You're cold, maybe because while you've been away you've grown out of your old winter coat, the sleeves are almost at your elbow. Your mother is scared, but she has your baby sister to attend to. You've taken so long to get to the car there's hardly any parking at the holiday sing. Your father has to park pretty far up a dark lane. *I'm not getting out of the car*, you say. Your father gets out, comes around, and pulls you out of the car by your collar. As he holds you up by the scruff of your neck, he props your crutches under your arms. *Now walk*, he says.

You stab at the frozen ground beneath the snow and swing your legs across the ice and make it to the magnolia tree just in time to sing the last verse of "Hark the Herald Angels Sing."

Glory to the newborn Creep.

~

SAY A MAN'S RELATIONSHIP to his God is determined by his relationship to his father. Your father memorizes Justin Wilson Cajun comedy records. He writes the jokes down and retells them to himself out loud when he thinks no one can hear him. He works on perfecting Justin Wilson's bayou accent. Your father is often paralyzed by his perfectionism. You read this in an evaluation you find going through his desk at home. Your father manages large forests and tracts of timber for a papermaking company. In his evaluation, your father's supervisor says he does an outstanding job but doesn't get as much accomplished because of his perfectionism. Also, the supervisor reports, your father's perfectionism creates problems with the men who work for him in the field. On your father's desk is a copy of *They All Discovered America*. Your father has a theory about what happened to the Lost Colony over on Roanoke Island, something to do with the grey-eyed Lumbee Indians down in Robeson County, North Carolina, where he has spent months cruising old-growth timber for the paper company. He's found an obscure account of a sighting of a white man, a white boy, and a mule down your town's own river in the sixteen hundreds. Your father has some questions for a professor at Duke and a librarian at East Carolina University, there are their telephone numbers and addresses on a notepad. In the bottom right-hand drawer of his desk are two coffee cans of arrowheads and spear tips he has found during hours of walking fields after fresh rains. He's thinking of buying some golf clubs, though he has never played golf. He has filled out an order form from a sporting goods company, and there is your mother's missing sewing tape that he's using to measure the length of his arms. In another desk drawer there are some dim grey photocopies of some ancestor's release from a Union prison near Vicksburg. He says two of your ancestors kicked a man to death in Sumrall, Mis-

sissippi, and fled to the relative safety of the Alamo; their names
are on the wall with those of the other patriots. Two of your other
relatives were caught in Pennsylvania stealing a locomotive for
the Confederacy and were hanged from a telegraph pole. Here
is an old photograph of five men hanging from a telegraph pole.
Here is a photo of a derailed steam engine alongside some broken
train tracks; someone has written in white marker with an arrow
pointing to spilled firewood nearby: *The bodies were found here.*
Here's an envelope with two mint-perfect Confederate currency
notes, a five and a ten, and two five-cent stamps with Jefferson
Davis's portrait. In the bottom left drawer of the rolltop desk are
the *Playboy*s, and on the top shelf of his closet, by where he keeps
the snake pistol, is the book you only flipped through once, having been stopped by the words urging the reader to remember to
pluck the woman's clitoris like a banjo string.

In a banker's cardboard box are maps and plats of the lake
property. Your father is going to subdivide the whole thing himself on weekends with a surveyor friend of his. You are no longer
on crutches, you can now walk with a cane, and your father says
you and an unemployed sharecropper he has found are going to
pull rod and chain for him down on the flooded Roanoke River
basin on Saturdays; the weather is still cold and there shouldn't
be too many snakes.

There are old wagon rut paths and ancient corn rows from
a hundred years ago grown over by pine and brush where the
valley falls off, and the footing is sharp, and you are no good at
pulling chain. You keep falling down and Mason, the sharecropper, keeps helping you back up. He doesn't understand how he's

supposed to balance the rod. Your father keeps stalking back and forth from point to point hacking at things with his machete. Mason lives in a large one-room house set on a clay mound. He's always ready when your father pulls up in front of the place, he meets you coming out the door, closes it quickly behind him in a way that even as a kid you understand that he's ashamed to let you see inside. He slaps on handfuls of English Leather that only partially cloak the smell of the house he shares with his wife and children.

When it's time to stop for lunch, your father has made a couple of peaunt-butter-and-fig sandwiches for you, but Mason doesn't eat lunch, says he isn't hungry, and you realize he didn't bring a lunch, so the next time your father doesn't bring a lunch either. You all drive to a colored country store, and your father buys lunch for everyone—little tins of Vienna sausages, cellophane cubes of saltines, slices of hard rat cheese the black man cuts off a block with a large knife, and RC Colas to drink. What you notice is how your father knows the owner of the little colored store and some of the black men who sit on the soft-drink cooler. Outside the store your father introduces you to a hundred-year-old black man sharpening a piece of metal on an old grinding stone. When your father's surveyor friend asks your father later how he knows the hundred-year-old man, your father says he gave him a ride home once. *He's a very interesting fellow,* your father says.

One morning your father pulls in to Mason's yard and a hound you've never seen before comes scramble-barking out from under the house. When Mason doesn't come out, you open your car door to knock. Dogs never bite you. You and your father are let inside the house by a woman who says she is Mason's wife. The single room is bright, lit by bare bulbs hanging from the ceiling. The windows are plastered over with newspaper. It's stifling hot from a woodstove, and smoky. Single beds are braced together, clothes are hung on long ropes. Things look like they've been blown against the walls by a tornado. When you look closely, there are faces in the piles of rags on the beds. Mason's wife is very sorry, but Mason is in the county hospital. Mason has gone insane. At the hospital they found that a roach had crawled into one of his ears and become stuck and died. The fluid built up behind the blockage and affected his brain. Mason went insane in the one room with his family for a few days before the eldest daughter could escape and fetch help.

You look at the eldest daughter. She looks older than her mother, but Mason told you once as you waited deep in the lake woods for your father to make his computations in his little surveyor's notebook that his eldest daughter is about your age. You look at her, and she stares straight back at you. Years later, when you hear she has become a witness for Christ in the Holy Land, you are not surprised.

FORTUNATELY, THERE IS AN OUT-OF-CONTROL FIRE in the Great Dismal Swamp that your father must see about and he decides to take you with him. Your father shows you the ditch George Washington surveyed to drain the swamp and the little railroad the loggers built to haul out the juniper logs. He shows you where he once saw a bear swimming the ditch with a cub on its back. He starts to tell you something about the tannic acid in the water of Lake Drummond when you come around a corner of the dirt road and see pumper trucks and firehoses abandoned and farther on, in thickening smoke, a lost school bus of frightened sailors from Norfolk who have been impressed into firefighting service. The wind has shifted, and they have panicked, the smoke pouring across the ground at them. Your father tries to explain to them that it is a peat fire mainly burning centuries of decay in the soil and that it probably won't hurt them, and right at that moment you hear some men shouting and you look over just in time to see a bulldozer being swallowed up in a deep smoky hole. See, your father says, the fire is burning *underneath* us.

Driving deeper into the smoke, you and your father pass more panicky people fleeing in the opposite direction. You arrive at Lake Drummond. Your father tells you the lake is a poquoson, the round water is actually higher than anything around it, like a coffee cup saucer turned upside down. *A meteor strike, probably*, says your father. It's a ghosty place and you like it, moss from the cypress trees, a black mood in the water, peat smoke blowing across it until you can't see very far and your eyes begin to burn and your father says, *We better get out of here*, and you do.

As you flee the fire, your father stops just ahead of the rolling smoke and crackling flames that are scalping the crowns of the trees, and you get out and take pictures of each other with a plastic camera you have brought. In one photo you stand on a little rusty railway handcar, the kind with the levers you pump to propel yourself along the tracks. You are pretending you are working the frozen levers trying to outrun the flames that are right behind you. Your father smiles as he takes your picture.

It is the best afternoon you will ever have in your life with your father.

⁂

THERE IS A SAWMILL and a paper mill in your town on the banks of a black-water river. You can hear the debarking drums turn all night stripping logs. There is sulfur in your air, and ash. Sometimes in the morning the ash lies thinly over everything, the mill has a free carwash to flush it off. The chugging smokestacks of the paper mill billow heavy white, day and night, mostly steam, they say. Some people think there's also something in the air that is an irritant to the central nervous system. From New York to Florida, people say, *I knew somebody from your town, and they was WILD.* From outer space, a new thermal heat picture shows a teardrop of warmth pluming up eastward from the smokestacks of your town, over Camptown, the colored shacks of the men whose forearms are blistered by stoking the boilers with coal and wood chips, whose lungs are ruined from unloading lime by the wheelbarrow from the bleach train, the janitors of the paper salesmen's offices. People say the warmth is the reason it doesn't snow so much anymore. Some people say your town stinks. Smells like money, is what your town says.

Jamestown is barely to the north, the town is full of its English ancestors, some Irish, some Huguenots. Richmond is to the northwest, close enough that on still days people could hear the cannons from its siege. The river through your town was Lee's last lifeline of food coming up in coasters from the Albemarle Sound. There is ancestor worship in your town. Quakers had spread abolition among the upper Baptists and lower Methodists and most had opposed secession, yet many rode off to join the fight for their own reasons, living in the saddles of horses for twelve days at the Battle of Brandy Station, three horses shot out from one of the citizens in one fight, one citizen shot dead the day before Appomattox. One officer for whom your street is named, finally finding his way home, to this county, this landscape and its women not as gang-raped by Union soldiers as others to the south, not having had as many typhus children's graves dug up by Union soldiers looking for buried silverware as others to the south, this one man coming home from seeing what he had seen and deciding to start the church where The Preacher preaches, this old Confederate officer finally just this emaciated thing in grey rags with a black gun-blasted face—his wife, an aged old lady now, turning and seeing, one day, a specter in her meager garden, and it is him, home again to a house that still stands on your street to this day.

To the east, the coast is so close seagulls wheel over freshly picked peanut fields, and softball themselves there in flocks to weather Atlantic storms. To the immediate south is the Carolina border, and the accents in your town are more Carolinian than Virginian, the open *o* vowel and the soft lift and glide of end-of-sentence cadence. To the southeast your river delivers its black swampy water to one and then another fresher, larger river that nourishes the tidal brackish Albemarle Sound and then is drawn by the tides through the Outer Banks beyond where the Elizabethans had set foot and then disappeared.

Since your grandmother has told your mother that she is going to hell, you will not be driving thirteen hundred miles that summer to Louisiana over unfinished interstate in the back of an un-air-conditioned car. You are twelve years old. Your dentist and his family invite your family down to their cottage on the Outer Banks for a week instead. The dentist lets air out of everyone's tires to drive up the sandy streets. You kids climb Jockey's Ridge, over one hundred feet tall, the tallest sand dune on the East Coast. Folklore says Satan is buried beneath it. You and the dentist's children take pieces of cardboard and sled down the gentle oceanside slopes, and you climb forever back up and stand on the dune's crest. Looking down on its sheer soundside back, you see the sand flooding through the windows of the abandoned houses as Jockey's Ridge migrates westward by the wind into Albemarle Sound. You are certain Satan is buried somewhere beneath your feet. The ominous white wind that lifts the pretty kites around you is also whisking away the mountain of sand that covers him. It feels as if Satan is buried here and he is not dead, merely sleeping.

In a shell and saltwater taffy gift shop, your father hands you a box. It is a ship-in-a-bottle kit. You look at it and you immediately know what it means, that when you get home from this vacation, you are headed back to Crippled Children's Hospital.

You know the routine; you wait to surrender yourself to the bed with the No Breakfast signs. You follow Nurse Wilfong on her rounds, help her as she tends to some of the younger boys. One day she asks you if you want a job, and you say sure, and she says go up to the office and raise the flag. She says she's noticed the flag hasn't been raised in a long time. There used to be an old scoutmaster who came by to make sure the flag was up every morning, but he doesn't come around anymore.

You go to the office and they give you the flag, and you go outside and raise it, and you look up at it for a long time. You go back inside the hospital, but you don't want to go back to the boys' ward, so you wander around. You go down the long hallway to Graham Ward, where the infants are. You walk around and look into cribs and see a lot of God's mistakes. There are things you probably should not see. You stare. A little baby girl reaches out to you, and there is only something like a crab claw on the end of her arm. In the next crib there's something that looks like it is from the bottom of an aquarium, but it is human and its eye follows you as you limp past. It is a loud crying place. It is a loud place of crying out. It is a place where you know a lot of the sounds coming out of the cribs are sounds calling for mothers. You suddenly miss your baby sister. Maybe you are crying and a nurse comes and walks with you all the way back to the boys' ward, miles and miles of red square tile.

WHEN YOU HOBBLE INTO HOMEROOM on crutches in the middle of fifth grade, you see your science poster on the wall. You had been warned by your tutor, the pretty lady with the large breasts, while you were home faceup and facedown in a body cast again. Besides the healing and decay in your body cast, you were also beginning to wake up with painful erections when your penis would inflate itself inside your plaster. Your pretty tutor with the large breasts that you could not look at had warned you about the science poster you were making at home showing the organs of the body, but you had not listened. You were determined to cut all the organs out of different-colored construction paper and paste them inside an outline of a human on a poster board, from the pituitary gland right down to the testes. Are you sure you want to include the reproductive organs as well? your tutor had asked. *Give me the scissors and a sheet of yellow paper, here are the testes,* you'd said.

When you hobble into homeroom in the middle of fifth grade, the first thing you see is your science poster taped to the wall, and someone has added in vivid ballpoint detail the large bulbous penis that had been missing.

On your crutches you do long solitary reconnoitering of your town, a stickly figure propped on a corner or in an alley or under a tree somewhere, sometimes in places where your mother would not be happy to find you. You watch feral cats fight over the fish guts behind Blow's Seafood Market, you rummage through the bins behind Leggett's department store looking for arms and legs to complete the mannequin you and your best friend are secretly assembling to dress in a trick-or-treating costume to throw in front of a car on Halloween. You wait behind the funeral home for the coroner's car to deliver a body. You listen to the people standing under the jailhouse windows talking up to the hands dangling out between the second-story metal bars.

You are on South Street in the black part of town when the Klan marches one Saturday, a bunch of men in cars with North Carolina license plates. Your police chief allows them to march only if they march without their hoods; he wants everybody to be able to see their faces. The men's faces are like those of any other men. Their robes are loose and blow open often. They wear work boots that clomp in unison at first until the sidewalk swells with jeers and hoots, and the boots almost break into a canting run, eager for their final destination, the Dairy Queen for hamburgers, where Cheryl the town prostitute takes their orders from behind the almost opaque Order Here window screen.

Maybe you are ranging too far in the gloaming late winter afternoons. You are dragging your legs between your crutches. One afternoon you are coming home at dusk along the sidewalk with your pockets full of worthless items you have shoplifted from Roses dime store when The Preacher pulls up across the street in his old blue station wagon. The Preacher gets out of his car with his books and his pipe and sees you paused in the walnut tree shadows. He starts to cross the street, and you wonder if he's already heard that you are stealing again. He comes over and lays a steadying hand on you, you hung on your crutches, and with you looking up and him looking down, he says only, *God has His hand on your shoulder*, before he crosses back to his house and heads inside for his supper.

It is in this fifth-grade year that for Show-and-Tell a boy from the county brings in a board with the piece of shellacked leather nailed onto it with small flat tacks. The leather is old and rough as he passes it around and lets everyone touch it. Nobody can guess what the item might be.

It's a piece of Nat Turner's skin! the boy says proudly.

It's a family heirloom.

The boy says that when they finally caught Old Nat in a cave of tree root out by his family's farm, they hanged him, cut off his head, and then some doctors skinned him and boiled him into fat. From the skin, people made little coin purses, Bible covers, and other souvenirs, like this piece of skin on a board.

Because you are on crutches and are slow, you are allowed to leave class five minutes early, the boy who runs the projector for science classes and has a ring of keys on his hip like a jailer helps you with your books. Out in the hall, the teacher is showing the principal the piece of Nat Turner's skin nailed to the board and they're wondering what to do. All you can think about is the time you watched some young doctors try to mend Michael Christian's red infected incision that had burst open in the bed next to yours.

Some of the houses where Nat Turner and his disciples killed people still stand derelict. Teenagers dare each other to walk through them at night. In one house there is still a large black stain on the floor where two women were decapitated. It is always cold in this house, even in July. When you are a teenager, you will walk through this house and come home covered in seed ticks after falling through a rotted floor.

Your history teacher tells your class that Nat Turner baptized a white man and that some people saw a white dove hover above them in the river. Nat Turner asked for signs from God, and he was given hieroglyphics on corn leaves. When he wanted more signs from God, he was given a green eclipse of the sun that was witnessed from Charleston, South Carolina, to New York City, so he and his disciples began killing as many white people in your county as they could, mostly with axes, swords, and hand tools. In two days they killed fifty-six people, most of them women and children, ancestors of many of your white classmates. Hundreds of blacks were killed in the weeks afterward, the ancestors of some of your black classmates.

Before they cut off Nat Turner's head and spiked it on a crossroads daring anyone to touch it, Nat sat in his cell and confessed that he was a prophet, a man of God.

THE SUMMER AFTER FIFTH GRADE you limp down to the black swamp riverbank, there's an old truck someone tried to drive into the water years ago. It's now just a hulk rusting deep in a ravine of blackberry bushes. You have to crawl through underbrush to get to it and climb in through the driver's window. The front fender is in the black water of the river creeping past. You can reach out and pick blackberries to eat right off the bushes and nobody knows where you are.

You are sitting down there one day behind the wheel eating blackberries and you faintly recognize a pattern on the old broken dashboard, the sun-corrupted leather split into squarish diamonds in a long pattern running the length of the dashboard, its triangular head moving toward you over the Sputnik-antennae turn signal jutting from the steering column, the split black tongue flickering, flickering, a sharp black bead of eye watching you as the water moccasin corners efficiently toward you from its hothouse sunning spot where the windshield creases into the dashboard. The only exit for you both is through the driver's side window, the snake's body now holding itself out firmly as a hurdle you must somehow with your skeletal legs superhumanly leap over to escape. Bracing your back so hard against the rusty springs of the backseat cushion in advent of your escape that you can feel them cut into your skin, you supernaturally fly out the driver's side window, your right kneecap rapping the snake's head with a bone-woodenish comic knock as you fly past.

After that your haunts are the library and the movie house. The library is in the old Pace family house, large enough so that the nine children roller-skated upstairs where the school board offices are now. There are hidden staircases and several sunporches. The place is haunted, not just by you or Miss Cutchins. Miss Cutchins knew your father didn't allow you to watch television when you were in your body cast, so she helped your mother select books for you to read by the grocerybagful. She will never deny you a book, though when you check out your books, *signing your name so that she can read it*, she will hold your book as if she can gauge its merit by its weight. Then she will inspect its spine, and if she is unfamiliar with the title, she might thumb through it while you lean on creaking crutches, if you are still on them, in front of her desk. She might read a few pages. She might deny a friend of yours a book until he is older, but never you, maybe because she knows you will slip off to one of the sunporches and read it anyway. She also knows that you will wait until *she* slips into one of the sunporches for her afternoon nap, that you will sign your name on the card so that she can read it, leave it on her desk, and swing your legs quietly out the door.

There had long been rumors of *Playboy* magazines in the closet behind Miss Cutchins's desk. One afternoon when Miss Cutchins is resting on the sunporch, and you could hear her resting out there, not quietly, you screw up your courage and open that closet door but all you find are years of your town's telephone books and Miss Cutchins's plastic rain bonnet.

When you confide to your best friend about your unsuccessful attempt to find a *Playboy* magazine, he tells you the solution is simple: all you have to do is go down to the bus station behind the queer real estate guy's office and steal one. The long afternoon you stand across from the bus station on your crutches you learn an important lesson: there are many great protections against temptation, and cowardice is one of the best.

The other person who haunts the old library is a Pace sister. She died a long time ago, and people think she is the reason books fall from the stacks, the broken clock in the main reading room chimes, and the front door sometimes opens and closes by itself. The librarians take the Pace sister's presence for granted. The people in the school board office upstairs aren't so sure, until in the middle of one of their meetings a woman came into the room, someone they thought at first must have been homeless and looking for the welfare office, her clothes were old and odd. When the secretary asked the woman if they could help her, the woman turned and disappeared into a wall.

Since then, they think they've identified the woman from an old photograph that is one hundred and forty years old. To this day, if you ask people who work in that building about the Pace sister, they usually say, *I don't know, I just know she seems to hang around that front parlor.*

Your other haunt is the movie theater owned by the alcoholic gay musician from Indiana who arrived first in a small Carolina town just over the border in a raccoon coat to play the enormous pipe organ they had installed in their movie house and nobody could get much music out of. People say he played at Radio City Music Hall and with the Mormon Tabernacle Choir. He's a nice man when he's sober. Sometimes when he's drinking, he bursts into the Saturday matinee in the middle of *Flipper* and chases children screaming into the street. You hang back and wait for him to climb the stairs to the projection room and see if the projectionist is able to talk him into going home. When you see the film begin to jump out of its sprockets on the screen into blinding whiteness, you figure it's time to go.

The projectionist lives on your street, and sometimes he lets you follow him down to open up the theater, and he lets you in for free if you help turn on the lights and start the popcorn, and you sit up in the Colored Balcony, the best seats in the house, where sometimes there's a party when the black children, who have to come up through an outside fire escape entrance, flatten popcorn boxes and send them sailing into the white audiences below.

Once, coming through the lobby, you tell the owner that was the best movie you have ever seen, and he says yes, Laurence Olivier is pretty good. Then he asks you if you would like a job there, and you say no, you and all of your friends have been warned away from the owner by parents. One Halloween, way after it was time for you and your best friend to be home from trick-or-treating, you found yourselves at his house loading up on the candy no one else had come to collect. The only people out on the streets were black teenagers throwing eggs and it was a long walk home. Your best friend called his mother, and when he told her where you were, she yelled, *I'll be right there!*

The woman who takes tickets at the movie theater says she's been raped by a black man and the police catch him. She never gives you back your change because you don't look twelve, she says you look too old for a kid's ticket. Without that ten cents you can't get any popcorn. You stop pressing her for the dime after she throws it at you saying, *Here!*

At that time, in your state, rape is a capital offense; you go to the Big House in Richmond, where they strap you into the electric chair. The Commonwealth's Attorney lives on your street, down three houses in the next block. The Preacher lives across the street with Janet and the boys. The Commonwealth's Attorney presses for the death penalty for the rapist and the jury delivers it. On the day the rapist is executed, The Preacher goes across the street and knocks on the Commonwealth's Attorney's door. When the Commonwealth's Attorney answers, The Preacher says, *Well, I hope you're proud of yourself.* The Commonwealth's Attorney says, *Yes, justice was served.*

In the years to come, the two men will barely speak.

In the years to come, you hear that the rapist had been extorting protection money from the poor blacks who lived in the neighborhoods behind you, neighborhoods from which the Commonwealth's Attorney collected rents. Janet will say that on Saturday nights The Preacher would be sitting in bed going over the next day's sermon, trying to ignore the singing and piano playing coming from the Commonwealth's Attorney's house across the street.

﹟

ONE MORNING YOU'RE SITTING at the dining room table and your
mother stands in the kitchen doorway and says she has water
boiling, what do you want for breakfast, soft-boiled eggs or oatmeal, and you croak, *Oatmeal.* Your voice has changed overnight.
It happens, your doctor says later, sometimes with choirboys,
boys from warm climates. Your mother almost drops her wooden
spoon and runs to fetch your father, who comes into the dining
room still holding the pair of square brushes he uses to get his
crew cut to stand perfectly up.

Tell your father what you want for breakfast, your mother
says, and you say *Oatmeal* again, this time even deeper. Your
mother looks at you with her fearful Catholic-lapsed eyes as if
your head might spin around and everything her mother has been
telling her is true.

Augie, the radio station manager who lives across the street,
tells your father that you could have a career in broadcast radio,
and your father wants to know if you can start right away. Well,
sure, says Augie, and pretty soon you are riding your bicycle
down to the little radio station in the strip mall by the river on the
edge of the black part of town.

The other announcers teach you how to pronounce the letter
W. You pronounce it *Double U.* Then they have you read some
news copy off the clattering UPI Teletype machine in the news-
room. They roll some tape, and you record your first commercial
for Leggett's department store, spring specials for men. When the
announcer who has the four o'clock show quits, Augie asks you

if you can get down to the station on your bike after school and
fill in. You'll have to get a work permit because you are underage.
The juvenile judge is willing to sign the work permit for you even
though your best friend's dog bit his son. It has been noted that
you are a surly boy and maybe this will straighten you out.

It is a small station located between a discount clothing store
for black people on one side and a beauty parlor and a Laundromat on the other side. Across the dogleg parking lot is a discount
drugstore and a supermarket, both patronized by black people.
The secretary of the radio station tells you to bring your bicycle
into the station in the afternoons, don't leave it out on the sidewalk.

There are two large turntables covered with green felt that is
replaced every time the town's saloon keeper puts new green felt
on his pool tables. Augie and the other salesmen ask the Lebanese
saloon keeper if they can have the scraps. Augie has said on the
air that the Lebanese saloon keeper is the only man in town more
popular than Jesus Christ. Augie can say things like that, he is
the voice of your town. When he introduces the black disc jockey
who follows him in the mornings to do the R&B show, Augie
says, *And now, in living color, Wally Hale!* After Wally Hale's
show, Augie comes back at noon to do the *Farm Hour*—crop
prices, weather forecasts, and the state of crop subsidies, which
your scoutmaster says are part of a larger Communist plot. After
the *Farm Hour* a lady who chain-smokes plays country music
until you arrive at four o'clock.

You play records from Augie's rack and some from Wally's,
you read the news off the Teletype machine, do Billboard of

the Air—mostly cakewalks, church dinner announcements, lost animals—read the final news, play the national anthem, and shut down the transmitter. You take out the trash, load the Teletype with paper, turn out the lights, lock the door, and then ride your bicycle home in the dark.

You make two dollars an hour.

Saturday mornings you no longer have to drag chain through the woods for your father, because you have the afternoon shift. If you need the whole day off to go camping with the Boy Scouts or participate in trash walks along the highway where once you found a fetus in a cider bottle, the other salesman with gouty feet can fill in, always happy to play the records from his days entertaining at the London USO Club during the war where he met his wife. His English wife doesn't understand his thrifty enthusiasms—spray painting their family car canary yellow with a box of aerosol cans he got in a convoluted radio commercial deal with a hardware store that was going out of business. Sometimes he turns the studio monitors up so loud that the hair dryers in the beauty parlor next door vibrate, and they hate to call but they do.

On Sunday mornings you all take turns hosting the *Gospel Show*. One Sunday a month you get up at five in the morning, ride your bike over to the cemetery, make sure the three red lights are burning on the antennae so you can check off the maintenance log. For a while there was a grave that broadcast the station, something to do with the metal lining of the burial vault and the fillings in the teeth of a lady's corpse, theorized the station engineer when some people from a television station came to investigate; then one day it stopped.

Then you ride through the sleeping town and open the station. You have to let the tube equipment warm up for a half hour and check the pile of Teletype that has been layering up all night. Vietnam. Patty Hearst. You used to have a crush on Jane Goodall but now you have a crush on Patty Hearst, the heiress who joined the Symbionese Liberation Army, after Jane Goodall never answered your letters. In your love letters to Jane Goodall you lied to her about the respect you had for what she was doing for all those monkeys. Secretly, you wanted to live with her in a tent with only books and a lantern among animals who walked comically worse than you do. On the transmitter, there is a series of flip levers and buttons to hold in for five seconds simultaneously and then release, knobs to turn just so to bring the station on the air, you're always nervous you'll get it wrong and blow up the transmitter. At 6:00 a.m. on the dot you pop in the cartridge with the national anthem played by the Air Force Academy orchestra. You're live, you're on the air, you're thirteen, good morning.

You watch carloads of black men pull up in the empty parking lot outside the studio through the large plate-glass window. There's the first preacher, a tight little man in a black suit, Bible under his arm. There's the Mighty Clouds of Joy, the Gospel Harmoneers, is that the Blind Boys? Some of the players, the guitarists and bassists, the keyboard musicians, have come straight from shot houses and roadhouses out near Four Corners or Checkboard Square or South Quay, they smell of cigarettes and gin, some are still a little drunk in sweaty yellow or purple faded tuxedo shirts with sprung collars and missing cuff links. They set up their equipment in the tiny B studio and make a lot of noise

you can hear in your headset while you've got the microphone
open reading the Darden Oil Company news.

You cue the little black preacher through the window to the
B studio and he welcomes all the brothers and sisters listening
and introduces the first hymn you're going to hear, already the
bass player is walking a few steps with his bass, and three or four
singers gather around the old standing microphone you patched
in as Augie showed you. You sit back at the console and trim the
levels and listen.

After the hymn, the preacher starts in with his good news
about the author of our salvation while the players clunk around
and whisper and open and shut the door and go out and get cold
drinks from the vending machines at the Laundromat. You study
the little black man who is off and running now, his eyes closed as
he preaches and starts ticking back and tocking forth in his chair,
his microphone is picking up the squeak in his chair and there's
nothing you can do about it. Watching this man through the
studio glass, you see that he is a believer. He believes in the hope
of redemption and in the promise of salvation. You lose track
of time. You let him run over. You wish you had his passion for
Christ Jesus. You think that someday you would like to be saved
as well.

※

THE FIRST TIME YOU ARE ARRESTED it is for assaulting a police
officer. Your parents and your baby sister are out of town. You
are on Main Street and it is a Saturday morning before you have
to go to work at the radio station. You stand between two parked

cars and shoot into traffic with a water pistol. Your best friend, David, comes along and wonders what you are doing. It's fun, you tell him. Here are some coins, go into Roses dime store and get a water pistol. *Get a big one*, you tell him.

Soon he joins you and here comes a police car. You reach out, almost into their car, and shoot the police officers in the face. Suddenly you are in the back of the police car driving one block to jail.

The two police officers bring you in front of the lieutenant. *You think this is funny?* asks the lieutenant as he empties the water pistol, squirting it in your face. They put you in a cell and slam the door. They probably already know about you, stealing lumber from behind the oil company, throwing crab apples at trucks, shooting that traveling salesman with navy beans through a blowgun.

Your best friend, David, makes what must be one of the longest walks of his life to the jail to turn himself in. When he appears in the jail doorway, the police grab him as if he is an escaped convict and throw him into the cell with you.

The Preacher is writing out a sermon when he gets the call from the police station. The Preacher says he can set his watch on Mondays after Sunday's sermon by the arrival of the delegation of little old ladies who have a problem with something in his sermon the day before. Sometimes the problems in the church have been about full immersion, because they are Baptists. Sometimes the problems are about an usher saying he will not seat a black person if one dares show up for service. To The Preacher, the answers to most problems reside in the answer to the question, Do you love your neighbor as thyself?

The Preacher's voice out in the police station sounds the way it does when it gives a blessing as it greets the police officers. Soon the jailer comes to get David. It has been hard to look at him because of what you have gotten him into. The jailer pulls David out of the cell and then slams the door shut and locks it. Not only are you going to miss work at the radio station this afternoon; you have to begin to think about spending the rest of the weekend in jail until your parents come home.

Then you hear footsteps. You look up, and The Preacher is standing with his pipe looking into your cell. He says to the jailer, *And I'll take this one too.*

The Preacher preaches that the end of pride is the beginning of forgiveness, that when a man in sincerity says *I have sinned,* it gives God a chance to say *I forgive.* The Preacher says that he is a sinner, that his witness is that of one beggar telling another where to find bread. The only sin you ever know him to commit is when he sometimes drives too fast up North High Street on his way home and gets caught in the speed trap by the cemetery. His sin is telling the policeman that the reason he was driving so fast was so that he could get to the hospital before visiting hours were over. Allowed on his way, The Preacher then invariably drives on to the hospital to give truth to the lie and perform little graces of comfort as afforded by the unwitting police department.

⁂

AT SCHOOL, A FIFTEEN-YEAR-OLD pregnant black girl sits with you in the back of social studies. She tells you names of new soul records her boyfriend brings her from Norfolk and you write down the titles of the songs. You have never seen skin as black as her skin; it is blacker than black ink.

Here is how someone has decided to integrate your school: you and half your class will go to the white high school in the morning, get on a bus at lunch, and then go to the black high school in the afternoon.

The first day of phys ed at the black high school you limp with your cane over to the bleachers to sit out baseball, but the black man everybody just calls Coach asks you, *Where you think you're going? Everybody plays.* Coach says all you have to do is knock the ball over the fence every time you go to bat. Coach has some old friends who used to play in the Negro Leagues. They come around and show everyone how to field and they show you how to hit. Your shoulders are broadening and your arms are strong from the years of crutches and pulling yourself around. With Coach pitching, you hit the ball over the fence, put down the bat, pick up your cane, and limp around the bases.

It's only you and three other white boys in phys ed. Some of the black kids are a lot older. Some of them shouldn't even be in high school. Some of them are worried about getting drafted to Vietnam. There is a butterball of a black boy named Willie who is very happy you are in his phys ed class. All his school life he has come in last doing laps, he is always the last to get chosen for teams. Now you come in last walking laps (because Coach says *Everybody does laps*) and you are the last person chosen for a team.

But on alternate days there is Your Health, and you are the

person all the students scoot their desks around on test days. Coach hands out the test and leaves to go check on something in the locker room. Everybody fights to get a look at your paper. You don't care. You lean back so they can get a better look as you fill in the blanks. Once, the assistant principal walked in and wondered what was going on, so now on test day you call out the answers as you fill in the multiple choice like you're calling out bingo—one A, two D, three C. When Coach comes back, everybody's finished, and for some of the boys Your Health is the only A they'll ever get in their lives.

You have to go in for some carpentry on one of your hips to rebuild a pelvic shelf with a bone graft. While you're laid up in bed with yet another body cast, Coach is the only person in the entire school system to come to your house to check on you.

YOU ARE SURPRISED THAT you still have a job at the radio station when you reemerge on crutches. Part of it is Augie, who likes you even though he doesn't like your music; part of it is the secretary telling the owner of the station that a lot of kids call in with requests when you are on the air, black kids, white kids, their calls give her a headache.

One girl keeps calling and says, *Play "Misty" for me*, then hangs up. *Play Misty for Me* is the title of an erotic thriller playing at the movie house. You listen harder to girls talking around their lockers at school, trying to figure out which of the two wallflower girls it is. It's either the first-chair flute in the school band or the girl who works at a pharmacy after school. A boy down the street confides to you that his older sister thinks your cane is sexy. You both stand there and look at each other confounded by this.

There are some older girls who, when they see you walking somewhere with your cane, stop their parents' car alongside the curb and say, *Get in.* Some of the girls have just gotten their driver's licenses. You think at first they feel sorry for you and are being nice, until the girls tell you they're going to pick you up that night and you will all go to a movie and then to the Dairy Queen and you say, Okay.

Sometimes the older girls take you to an R-rated movie, and then they ride around out in the county smoking cigarettes in their parents' big Buicks. It's three of them in the front seat and just you in the back with your cane and they seem to forget you're back there as they talk about who's horny and who's having their periods. It's nighttime, so they can pick up a radio station in Chicago as you drive around and smell the dark county in bloom with the windows down if the bugs aren't bad, the honeysuckle and the bubbling swamp gas smell of rotting vegetation.

There's an older girl who goes to your new church, red hair that burns crimson in the stained-glass light; even your mother has commented on the girl's hair, long, gold, highlit with garnet when you sit in the pew behind her and her family in your father's church. After the incident with the drunken, rope-wielding priest, God for your mother had been a Ouija board, then astrology, then a book of physical fitness published by the Royal Canadian Air Force. You are relieved to be no longer Catholic, even though you are probably going to hell with your mother. When your father called Catholic Communion "The Magic Show," you laughed out loud.

You like your new church, your father's Episcopal church, and you like the new priest, Ben. The church smells good, old wood, fresh starch, and the cologne and expensive perfume of the Whiskeypalians, as some of the Baptists call them. The old church organ was brought over from England in the hold of a sailing ship. You like to sit near the man in the sharp suit who defended the spy pilot Gary Powers when he was shot down over Russia in his U-2. His wife is the sister of the poet laureate of the state. There's the new paper mill manager and his pretty wife, both from Richmond society. Elizabeth Taylor stays at their house when she's in town with her husband, who is campaigning for the Senate. After service, many will congregate and smoke outside the vestibule steps. Some will go directly to the country club for lunch and discuss Ben, the new priest. Some parishioners find him a little liberal for their tastes. Ben retired as a decorated Air Force fighter pilot before entering seminary to become a priest. When he hears that "somebody" said that he might be a bit liberal, Ben says to tell that "somebody," *Yes, I am a liberal and I am combat ready.*

The church has a coffeehouse in the parish hall on weekend nights for kids to gather for fellowship. Black-light posters and a pool table, parent chaperones in the back. It's a place kids meet and get in cars and go out into the nearby woods to smoke pot and drink beer and do the things teenagers do.

The older girl with the brilliant hair has been meeting you at the coffeehouse and letting you take her into a nearby alley because you don't have your license, and the older girl lets you do pretty much whatever you want as long as you are standing, or she only has to kneel to do it. In church you realize that the perfume you come home with on your clothes must be her mother's, because once at the Communion rail you knelt beside her mother and smelled it and your heart beat faster. When you glanced sideways at the mother as she opened her mouth and slightly extended her tongue to accept the little white sliver of host, there was a knot of confusion in your pants.

A MAN AT THE POST OFFICE tells you your father is a real crack-up. You're finding out your father is doing stand-up comedy in hunt clubs out in the county and down in North Carolina. He's been doing the Justin Wilson records there and people ask him back. Then you hear your father is in a play somewhere, he has the lead.

Your father has a lot of things going on. Your mother is worried that he has bought new underwear. He says he is going to work at the lake property and forgets his tools. His car is hit by a watermelon truck going the wrong way on a one-way street, your father says he didn't see it coming. He doesn't realize school is out, that you're just spending your days in the backyard hammock reading Ambrose Bierce short stories and histories of the navies of the world.

But your mother notices and signs you up for advanced-placement math class out at the high school. You're always late, stopping on your bike to listen to the cornstalks grow and pop in a cornfield. It's so hot the pavement is splitting open and you have a spectacular bike wreck, going over the handlebars and sprawling on the sticky tarmac. One of your legs won't stop quivering, like the time you fell at Crippled Children's and they called the doctor's stat and Charles knelt beside you, your spasming leg bouncing off the floor until you yelled *Hit it with a rolled-up newspaper!* and Charles started laughing and the spasming stopped, and your leg rolled over exhausted and went to sleep.

The advanced-placement class bumps you that fall into an algebra class taught by a teacher who polices with a meter stick she once broke over a slow country boy's back. She looks at you, the youngest in the class, a cripple too, and she smells a cheat.

In defining finite and infinite numbers, she says, by definition, finite terms are numbers assigned to things that can be counted. For instance, is the number of grains of sand in Jockey's Ridge finite or infinite? You're the kid holding his hand highest to be called upon, eager. You say the number of grains of sand in Jockey's Ridge is infinite. Miss Meter Stick smiles and says, No, if you could count them, you would find that there is a finite number of grains of sand in Jockey's Ridge. No, you say, that's incorrect. First of all, you patiently explain, the ocean is constantly throwing up fresh sand that dries and is blown onto the dune by the wind at the same time the same wind is carrying sand off the dune into Albemarle Sound. Second, you say, even as you notice Miss Meter Stick tapping the meter stick against the side of one of her shoes, her smiling face beginning to purple, second, the number of grains of sand in Jockey's Ridge would have to be considered infinite by her very own definition of being able to count them; if the grains cannot be counted, there is no finite answer, hence no finite number. But if you *could* count them, she says, as she moves down the aisle of seats to where you are seated, you would eventually reach a number, a *finite* number, so you're wrong, she says, poking the corner of your desk with her finger. Then *you* go fucking count them, you unwisely counter, and you are sent home from school for two days at a time when your father is toward the end of his first affair and is looking for someone upon whom to vent his guilt. You had long before nicknamed his backhands "flying tigers" after his college mascot, Mike the Tiger, whose tiny head ornamented the LSU class ring worn on the hand delivering the often unexpected blow.

You avoid your father and in the Indian summer evenings read William Faulkner's *Light in August* in your stuffy second-story bedroom. The pages soak with your dripping sweat. You don't understand a lot of the book and it doesn't matter, you concentrate on the pages anytime your father passes your door. As in the book, your town has a mysterious black man living in an old unheated house without plumbing in the woods on the edge of town. People call him Hogbear, and he roams your town in the day foraging for food from the rancid trash behind supermarkets. His bicycle is adorned with streamers and bits of colored cloth, the seat levered up to its highest position, the handlebars extended with sawed-off broomsticks. He wears a military jacket with sergeant stripes on the sleeves and a military cap. He says he won World War II by hitting a bull's-eye on a rifle range in Illinois. He rides his bike back and forth to Norfolk, and he'll come down off the bike when children throw rocks at him and call him Hogbear. His real name is Robert, Robert DeLoatch, and your father tells you when you see him behind the radio station going through the trash to be polite and call him Mr. DeLoatch, and this is what you do.

As in the book, your town has many spinsters living in old houses, like the old sisters who live two blocks over on High Street, where you go to sell lightbulbs and cleaning brushes to earn money for Boy Scout camp. They were up on the third floor of their house when you knocked, and there was that strange small ball of light circling the ceiling. One sister sat in a corner, and the other, the one who had urged you up the two creaking flights of dark steps up through the unlocked front door when you knocked, the low-simmer smell of something old stewing somewhere, the one who had urged you up made a gesture with her wrist and finger following the small ball of light circling the ceiling. The look on her face was that it would all be explained later, and you realized, as you fled fearfully down the stairs, your cardboard sample suitcase of lightbulbs and cleaning brushes dumbling down beside you, that she meant that it was all explained in the past, as in the book you are reading. As in the book, people learn, as you are learning, that some things can never be explained, like that strange light circling the ceiling, even when you run to The Preacher's house and tell Janet and she says that everyone *knows* that house is haunted.

As in the book, people in your town want to make examples out of others, you even see it in yourself, the teachers who want to make an example out of you, because maybe that is the flip side of mercy toward the crippled. There's another teacher at your school who keeps you off the honor roll by giving you a C in handwriting, for which a flying tiger will spring from the ceiling. When it is time to separate the college-bound from the vocational-skills students in your class, the teacher takes you all on field trips to show you the importance of an education. She takes you to a windowless, airless basement of a peanut warehouse with unbreathable peanut-dust air lit by a dim red lightbulb to witness the example of an old black man with a hoe guiding an endless stream of peanuts onto an endless conveyor belt that disappears into a black hole in a wall. She shows the example of the old man at the sewage plant sweeping spent condoms and rock-hard turds off the top of the bubbling brown settling pool of sludge with a long-handled swimming pool scoop and dumping them in a bucket. *See?* she will hiss.

Your father finally comes into your room one night as you read your book. He has something to tell you. He says the paper mill is digging four new wells on the river, they need more water for the papermaking process. People's wells have been going dry, the water table has dropped for ninety miles around. Your father says where they're digging the wells is the site of an old Indian camp. He says he bets you could probably find a lot of arrow-heads if you look.

You and a friend go over where the drillers are unearthing thousands of years of human habitation and dumping it in piles the size of your house. You find some nice arrowheads and relics, including a ceremonial bowl shaped from a mollusk fossil. The fossil is four or five million years old, from a time when all of this land was underwater in a shallow ocean. You know this is true because you have gone out in the country and stood on the special little bridge a man built over his creek, and you have looked down over the rail and seen that the creek runs through the fossilized spine and splayed rib bones of a whale trapped in rock that must be as old as God.

You finish reading *Light in August* and you don't understand a lot of it and it doesn't matter. You are learning that time doesn't always move forward, sometimes it moves backward, and that is a great comfort when you know exactly how many months and years it will be before you are committed to a wheelchair forever.

\|//

YOU'VE HEARD PEOPLE SAY God gave us the moon and the Devil gives us its moods. You've taken to roaming the countryside on moonlit nights with a boy of whom your mother is especially suspicious. His family lives near you, his little brother and sister, twins, come around asking for work, and your mother gives them jobs you no longer do around the house. She hires them to rake the leaves from the large oak tree in your backyard, then she overpays them and gives them more lunch than they can eat later. Their father has an old van that he has cut down to move lumber. He has taken out all the seats, there is no glass in the windows, there are no headlights, no license plates, the van is not supposed to leave the premises. It's a banged-up vehicle that expels thick grey smoke when you finally get it started, so your friends call it the Smokebus, at least that's the first reason they call it the Smokebus. On moonlit nights, because there are no headlights by which to see the roads, you and your friends throw some lawn furniture in the bus, and whoever is driving straps on some safety goggles to drive because there is no windshield and the bugs are fierce when you drive through the swamps, and you set out toward the pig farms in the northwest part of the county to steal a baby pig. There is a black shot house in the opposite corner of the county called Miss Pearl's and if you bring Miss Pearl a baby pig in a burlap sack and put it in her pigpen out back, Miss Pearl will give you underage drinkers either a case of beer or a pint of whiskey.

Full-grown sows can weigh a quarter of a ton and more, and if they knock you down, they can kill you and eat you. They are protective of their young except when they accidentally step on them; that is why they have so many in a litter. The mud and pig slop is slippery in their pens, and you can't run fast, you can't run at all. Somebody brings a softball bat and you think that is a good idea. Occasionally, a light will come on and a shotgun will be fired in your direction, over your heads, but that is rare.

Your friend whose father owns the Smokebus has long blond hair parted in the middle, broken teeth, and a laugh that sounds like he is choking. He wears an old long raincoat and a dirty driving cap. One night he says there's not enough gas to take the long way around town. He says the Smokebus is invisible because it has no lights, so he's going to drive straight through town as fast as he can. There are two stoplights in town and you are stopped behind a log truck. Everyone is muddy and it is your turn to hold down the burlap sack with the screaming pig fighting to escape. The Smokebus is coughing and rocking as the pig gets halfway out of the burlap sack. It is not a baby pig, more like a juvenile. You are all trying to stuff the pig back into the burlap sack, the van is rocking as you and the others chase it around, banging and falling over the upended aluminum lawn furniture. In the middle of it all you look out the paneless window, and you see your father has pulled up alongside you in his car and he's looking over at what in the hell is going on over there in that van. Your and your father's eyes meet for several long moments, and the way he turns and looks straight ahead you understand that he does not see you where you aren't supposed to be doing what you're doing, because he is on his way to where he is not supposed to be going to do something he is not supposed to do.

Something dark settles over these ventures and you don't ride with them for a while. People out in the county are talking about the pig rustling, more shots are fired. The next time you ride along, somebody brings a rifle, and you decide this is the last time you are doing this. There's not much of a moon, there's barely enough light to see, and when you pass through the swamp bottoms, whoever is driving has to look up and follow the grey swath of sky through the tops of the trees to stay on the road.

You are the one who shoots the church. There had been random shooting out the Smokebus window and careless gun handling by others. The rifle had gone off and put a hole in the floor by one of your feet. Clouds are confounding the moon, it's past time to go home. You grab the rifle away and decide to empty the clip at the next lights you see and it's the marquee and steeple lights of an old church, and you unload the rifle in the church's direction and you're done.

Years later you'll stop and walk around the church like a tourist because in local history the church is famous as a hot pulpit of abolition before the Civil War. You walk around the church pretending to admire it all the while looking for bullet holes. You don't see anything except some holes up in an eave that could just be carpenter wasps.

For your sins you get hard knots, two nodules pressing up under your skin chafing red beneath your belt with the CSA buckle. It's the heads of two nails in a mending plate in your right hip that are working themselves out of your bones. The doctor decides he can take the nails out of your hip without putting you to sleep. Your father drives you to Richmond and they put you on a table. Two orderlies hold you down. The surgeon gives you a shot of local anesthesia in your hip. A nurse holds your head so you won't look. The surgeon cuts into your skin and has a hard time getting the nails out. He has to get some pliers to pull the nails out, and he almost pulls you off the table. It's not so much the pain, it's the squeaking of the nails in your bones as he has to twist them back and forth like he's pulling them out of wet lumber. It's also the way the nurse winces and the way the doctor grunts with the effort. It looks like you'll be going back into the hospital the next summer. When it's over and you're sitting in your father's car in the parking lot, he asks you if you want a pastrami sandwich. You wish you could ask him for a cigarette and a beer. When he asks if you're okay, you say, *Let's just go home.*

THE BEST THINGS ABOUT your last year in your town after the last body cast and the crutches again are a girl, a play, and a short story. This girl is another redhead, bright blacklit brass, and she is the editor of the school newspaper. She's a little older than you and asks you to write humor pieces for the paper. She reads them, laughs, and hands them back, saying, *You're crazy, I can't print this*. Instead, she teaches you to drive a stick shift, and you drive you two out to that fallen tree way out by the millpond.

In town her parents are elderly and have arthritic knees and can't get up the attic steps that you can only slowly navigate on your crutches while the girl smiles and waits at the top, unbuttoning her shirt. Up in the attic is a dormer window that swings open onto limbs of green branches and bright blue sky, and there are old mattresses up there, and you can take all the time that you feel you have left with her. She has drawn blood on your upper lip with her teeth; she gives you raspberry hickeys that horrify your mother and make some of your girl classmates wonder who, who would do that to a boy on crutches?

There's another best thing of a drama teacher who casts you in the lead as Mr. Antrobus in *The Skin of Our Teeth*, compelling you to get off your crutches and cane early, and there's the English teacher who pushes you and pushes you to finally write a comprehensible term paper, and if you can't do that, then a short story will suffice, and you write a story called "A Case of Eggs," and she enters it into a regional short story contest and it wins. When your teacher hands it back to you, the community college judge has written "seeds of excellence" on the cover page.

AFTER THE WAR, ROBERT E. LEE became headmaster of a small academy, and that is where you go to college. They've saved Lee's desk as it was on the day he died, writing a letter to the parents of a slothful student. In photographs you see Lee dressed in suits cut from his old grey uniforms. You are required to wear a coat and tie to some of the classes, and this place might not be the best fit for you, you with your shoulder-length hair and bib overalls and records by the thousands you haul up there that don't sound anything like the beach music most of the prep school boys seem to listen to.

Your new best friend is a boy from Houston, Texas, with a melted face from an explosion and you know each other very well on the day you first meet. Your other friend is from Roanoke, Virginia, and he has a 1955 bulletproof limousine that his father bought from the Turkish embassy, and in it you make the rounds of girls' schools and ease into parades with little flags put on the bumpers, him driving, you in the back waving to crowds and in a coat and tie.

You get a job working for the literary magazine, and the editor, Jim Boatwright, invites you and the other young assistant to his home to listen to Bessie Smith records and gives you a dinner of chicken livers. Later, he wants to know if you want to go downstairs and have a steam in his sauna. The other young assistant does but you don't, and Boatwright keeps you on the staff anyway. He teaches creative writing, and it's the only A you get your first year in college. Once, when Walker Percy comes to visit, Boatwright asks him to sit in on your class, and you read a story called "The Moon Struck One"; it is about the night you and David were frog-gigging and you reached down and were struck on the hand by a snake, you were in a nest of snakes in the dark, and the part of the story Walker Percy tells you he likes best was when the best friend tells you it's okay, he was bitten too, and he holds his hand up for you to see, but you can't see it, because it's dark. Boatwright also introduces you to Reynolds Price when he comes one afternoon in a brand-new brown leather jacket, before he was stricken, and you read *The Surface of Earth*, and all you want to do at the college is take writing courses and work at the college radio station. You sign up for prelaw, but with your grades, it's like they say, the back door of the Commerce School is the front door of the Journalism School, so that is where you spend your time, there and in the English department proofreading for the literary magazine and sorting post office bags when it's time to ship issues.

You tag along when they go down to Roanoke to pick up Truman Capote at the airport, and the first thing he wants is a drink, and the only place your friend with the limousine knows is the Polynesian restaurant by the airport where they serve birdbath-sized drinks with fruit and parasols, and Mr. Capote says, *Perfect!* You're supposed to keep an eye on the time because you still have an hour drive to school, but Mr. Capote keeps ordering scorpions, and you're all getting drunk listening to him talk about a man who injected rattlesnakes with amphetamines and put them in a car that someone got into and the doors locked once he got in and he was bitten to death, isn't that something? *It's true, it's true!* he keeps saying in a catlike voice; he says he has the newspaper clippings to prove it.

By the time you get to the school auditorium for the reading, people are leaving, and there are some people really angry with you. Mr. Capote has requested a pink spotlight, and even though he's had as much to drink as you, he goes right to the podium and gives a reading of a Christmas story that makes people cry. Afterward, he signs two books for you; one you give to the father of a girl you are in love with who will die. She will be your first true love. When you would drive out to her gentleman farmer's house, you'd take bunches of gardenias cut from your neighbors' bushes, and while you'd wait for her to get ready, you and her father would sit on the back patio if it wasn't too buggy; his house was near the river where you could still see trenches from the siege of Suffolk, and the two of you would talk books, Faulkner and Camus. For years after she dies, when you would run into each other, you both try not to cry.

Your other writing teacher is an angry man who has just come from flying reconnaissance missions over the Ho Chi Minh Trail, and it is in his class that you begin writing a series of stories about a character you name the Spotlight Kid, cribbing the title from a Captain Beefheart song. The teacher's office is empty of books, his shelves are bare, as if he knows he is just passing through, and he is, but not before he reaches into a cardboard box beside his desk and gives you books by Richard Brautigan, Thomas McGuane, and Louis-Ferdinand Céline.

YOU HAVE COME TO A POINT at your private coat-and-tie college where the dean has asked you to come to his office for yet another talk. To cover your impending exit, you intern with a small weekly newspaper in Virginia Beach during spring semester. There's the beauty pageant where you don't behave well and the terrifying ride in a Blue Angels F-4 that permanently bursts some blood vessels in your left eye. You wreck your car several times, an over-powered Mercury Montego MX. The last article you write is this: the circus has come to town, and you spend the day watching the wranglers use the elephants to hoist the tent poles and canvas. Later, you see a guy bathing out of a bucket, and you think, *That's the life for me!* as you face another college-boy summer in the paper mill and having to tell your father that the dean of the college has invited you not to return to school the next fall.

BUT THEN YOU GET THE CALL. David and your other best friend, Steve, are camped in a World War II Army tent pitched in a five-dollar-a-night campground on Roanoke Island. Bug-bit, down to their last twenty, living on peanut-butter-and-honey sandwiches, sleeping in the sweltering tent at night stitched up against the black swarms of tiger mosquitoes, bruising each other with sleeping-bag punches thrown in the dark over snoring. Every day they go down to Wanchese to get on a scallop boat, having heard you could make as much money in one week on a scallop boat as you could all summer in the paper mill. And they had believed it. When they discover the depth of the deception, they call you collect, them snickering, broke, bug-eaten, and wild-eyed hungry beneath the campground pay-phone streetlight, and they sell you the same story, and you believe it.

No one will lead you down a slippery path faster than your best friends. They know how much you hate the idea of working graveyard shifts in the paper mill, where your fathers are white-collar management, and where the blue-collar labor enjoys assigning college boys home for the summer double shifts unloading pulpwood off river barges, breaking up logjams on the conveyors with long-handled picks more effectively used to fend off the thigh-sized water moccasins that came slithering along with the cargo.

So you drive down to Roanoke Island, stopping for gas at the country store where a man kept a bear in a cage out back. One summer, with a bladder full of eighty-nine-cents-a-six-pack A&P beer, you'd stumbled behind the store after finding the men's room occupied and had a pretty good torrent going into a stand of bamboo when the bear came charging within inches of you, the cage bars hidden in the thicker stalks of cane. When your friends in the car wondered what had taken you so long and why you had pissed all over your pants and shoes, you just shook your head and told them to drive.

Currituck County, your last step before crossing the sound on into Dare County, is still full of black bears, they say, especially up and down the Alligator River. You know a man who one night set out to kill the bear that was destroying his vineyard, and as in a fable he fell asleep around midnight with his shotgun across his lap. He woke up hearing grunting and thrashing paws ripping clusters of grapes, and he smelled the smell of bear, strong, he said. He stood up, and the bears stood up, one by one around him, five of them, checking out the interloper. Later you tasted the man's wine, and he was right: nothing to kill a bear over.

You have about two hundred dollars when you find your

best friends in their campground, and they take the money and buy some Rebel Yell bourbon and a cheap motel room. The next morning you use what is left to rent a Nags Head beach cottage that the week before had been scheduled for bulldozing. The two hundred dollars isn't really yours to spend; you were supposed to have given it to the lady in whose basement you'd been living in Virginia Beach, but while she had been away, you let some surfer friends and their girlfriends stay in the house, and some things had gotten messed up, so you had left without saying goodbye.

Here is how the Wanchese scallop boats assemble their crews. You work for free getting the trawler ready to go fishing, changing over gear, painting, rerigging, building dredges, and then after the tons of ice are shoveled into the hold, the captain says, *You, you, and you.* If you've worked hard, maybe you and about ten other guys will get on. This doesn't sound like a good idea, but by this time all the paper-mill jobs had been filled. What seemed more sensible was to approach a man who had caught you all asleep in some cottages you had broken into the previous spring in Kill Devil Hills and ask him for a job. Instead of calling the police, he had put you to work opening his restaurant, painting, scraping oven grease, nailing in new screens, and shoveling tons of sand out of the parking lot. He didn't pay you but said you had done a good job. This idea is vetoed by your friends. Besides, they say, remember on the last day everyone was working for the man and you realized it was Easter Sunday and excused yourself and hitchhiked to church? He's not going to hire you, they say, he thinks you're some kind of weirdo. Okay, you say.

So you start working on the docks for free, and pretty soon

you're down to peanut-butter-and-honey sandwiches. You all get on the phone and call another friend of yours collect and tell him about all the money you can make working on a scallop boat in one week, and a couple of days later Ricky arrives. Ricky has some money his aunt had given him, so you all take that and buy some Rebel Yell bourbon and set up the tent behind your cottage and then light it on fire. Later that night you take the charred wooden tent poles and beat one another with them, yelling, *Kung Fu!* accidentally knocking Ricky unconscious. You drag him into a spare room and feed a lawn sprinkler from a realty office next door in through the window and turn it on full blast so that Ricky can wake up.

Finally, the most notoriously violent Wanchese captain of all, with a single name known from Mexico to Rhode Island, a large burly man with an enormous black beard that creeps all the way up to his shocking blue eyes, taps two of you to join his crew. You and Ricky go.

It was either that trip or the next that you go to your first and only whorehouse. The captain and the cook wanted to go, everybody else wanted to go to the discos near the docks in Cape May. Okay, you'll go to the whorehouse, you thinking it'll be like in the movie *Paint Your Wagon* with Jean Seberg and girls in garters and bustiers. Your captain steals a fish truck, and you drive down and past the smell of rotting fish and pull in to a trailer park. The girls are ugly and nice. One of them takes your captain into the way back of the trailer, and other girls want to know which of the girls in the kitchen do you want to have a "date" with? You like the one shuffling cards at the kitchenette table, she could almost be the sister of the girl you starred with in *The Skin of Our Teeth*, but instead you ask, what are y'all playing? Spades. So for a few hours you and she and two other girls play spades and drink vodka and smoke some roaches from the ashtray and listen to Lynyrd Skynyrd and have a party. The big girl who took your captain comes out and says, Your captain is *tired*.

Nobody else comes to the trailer that night, and later you and the girls all pass out just like normal people. At dawn some guy, maybe their manager or pimp, comes and shakes you where you're sleeping on the couch. He's an older guy, maybe even thirty. He wants to know what you're doing there, and one of the girls who passed out on the recliner wakes up cranky and says to leave you alone, you're not a john, and your captain comes out just then like a big bear growling out of hibernation, and the pimp backs off, and when you and your captain get into the fish truck, you realize you could have driven yourself back that night after all, that there is just a screwdriver jammed into the ignition.

✧

DURING WORLD WAR II, German U-boats sleeked up and down the Outer Banks, unchallenged in the early days, sometimes sinking ships at the rate of one a day—oily smoke on the horizon and the bodies of seamen washing up onto the beaches to be found by schoolchildren. From the decks of the scallop boats, you often dredge up the cargo Churchill fretted after. On one trip you and your crewmates pull up hundreds of helmets, the webbing rotted out, and you all wear them until one comes up with the top part of a skull affixed to the inside, and everyone heaves them overboard.

The crew looks for old torpedoes in the nets and dredges as they are swung aboard. People were still talking about the live torpedo that slid out of the scallop boat *Snoopy*'s nets, killing eight of the twelve crew members aboard. Once, miles over the horizon from shore, your trawler pulls up several ossified motorcycles that seem chiseled out of cheap concrete.

As a cub reporter in Virginia Beach, you had interviewed the Navy diver who explored the first U-boat sunk in U.S. waters in the war, U-85, just off Bodie Light. It had been a messy kill. An old World War I destroyer, pressed into patroling the coast, caught the sub on the surface one night trying to put men ashore, or so the diver believed. The destroyer punched holes in the U-boat's conning tower with its three-inch gun, then raked its deck with machine-gun fire. No one is certain if the U-boat was submerging or sinking stem first into the April waters. German sailors abandoned ship and began calling for help. Fearing a trap and perhaps feeling a rage, the destroyer depth-charged every-thing, settling the U-boat in a hundred feet of icy water, its dead blue crew retrieved, all internally ruptured.

The old Navy diver tells you that on his first daylight descent to the U-boat the first thing he saw, painted on the conning tower, was a wild boar with a red rose in its mouth. He said the way the sun struck it, it was a beautiful sight underwater that he would never forget. In the sub's compartments he found bodies and thousands of U.S. dollars floating around like large confetti. Of the twenty-nine bodies recovered, four were in civilian clothes, and souvenir hunters aboard the recovery vessel found American Social Security cards and driver's licenses in the pockets. The

U-boat crew members were secretly buried in their underwear in numbered graves in the National Cemetery just north in Hampton, Virginia. To the south, on Ocracoke Island, four British sailors, U-boat victims, are buried in a small cemetery where every year a fresh Union Jack arrives punctually from the Queen.

※

HUNDREDS OF SHIPWRECKS LITTER the ocean floor off the Outer Banks, most stranded and beaten to pieces on Diamond Shoals off Cape Hatteras, where the cold Labrador Current collides with the warm waters of the Gulf Stream on their way to take the chill off the Swedish reindeer cowboy's winter above the Arctic Circle.

From the dredgings, you collect smooth river-stone ballast, imagining the English streams from which it had originated, until there was just too much of it and you toss it over the side. The smaller items are more interesting, the handmade bottles and the clay trading pipes, some long-stemmed sorts remarkably intact and functional off-watch, in the forepeak packed to the brim with Roanoke Island homegrown. Foolishly, you let the other winch man on your watch use your best pipe once. A sudden turn in the rudder sent the holder pitching over; the pipe fell to the floor and shattered; your curse at losing the pipe was matched by the curse coming from the bunk below—he hadn't gotten his hit yet.

※

YOUR FATHER TRIES TO FIND YOU in your condemned cottage a couple of times when you're out at sea. Once, he finds Ricky, lounging in the living room, covered in flies and reading Edgar

Allan Poe, bong nearby, Ricky oblivious to the incessant buzzing and crawling. A three-foot lobster that had come up in your nets was rotting under the front porch. Your father never tells you he'd been there, had seen the way you were living. He told Ricky to tell you that he dropped by, but Ricky "forgot."

Here is a Ricky Illustration. One night, getting ready to go to the dance pavilion, you and your best friends accidentally take some pills you have found and wake up several hours later when Ricky comes in and announces, *Hey, somebody stole my car!* Somebody stole your car? *Yeah*, he says, kind of crazy-eyed, *that guy right over there!* He points to a little stilted cottage diagonally across the beach road where a friendly dope dealer lives. You and your buddies kick open the dope dealer's door and put him by the throat against the wall. *Where's Ricky's car?* you all demand. When he can take a breath, the dope dealer says just a little while earlier he had picked up Ricky, who was walking along the side of the road from the dance pavilion. Evidently, Ricky had experienced another of his infamous blackouts at the dance pavilion, wandered out the beach exit instead of the road entrance, and, unable to find his car in the wrong parking lot, was walking up and down the beach road disoriented until the dope dealer recognized him and offered Ricky, a good customer, a ride home. *Is that true?* you all demand. The dope dealer pointed out that if he'd stolen Ricky's car, why isn't it parked under his cottage? In fact, the dope dealer was pretty sure the car is still in the parking lot of the dance pavilion. Turning to Ricky for his side of the story Ricky suddenly stares down at his bare feet and exclaims, pointing, *Hey, somebody stole my shoes!*

It is probably a good thing that Ricky returns to college at the end of the summer to complete his business degree and become a captain of industry. Everyone seems to be returning to school except you and Steve. You've made a lot of money and have spent every penny. There is no college money—a moot point, since your college has invited you not to return that semester. The first mate on the scallop trawler you crewed on is a guy named Art. He and his best friend are looking for an extra hand to take an old wooden subchaser down the Intracoastal that fall, en route to the Caribbean. You have just read Thomas McGuane's *Ninety-two in the Shade* and you want to see the Florida Keys. You drive home to sell it to your father as a once-in-a-lifetime opportunity to cruise the Caribbean, much like the time he had spent smoke-jumping in Idaho. Your father listens patiently, sipping from his green goldfish bowl of ice and Rebel Yell bourbon. Finally, he says he will make a deal with you; he will give you his blessing if you promise to finish college the next year, on the condition that he will no longer have to foot any part of your tuition. You jump at the bargain. Driving down to Nags Head later, you catch the hook in your father's proposition. You are still smarting from your mother's parting comment to you. When she had finished your summer's worth of laundry, boiled and line-dried, especially the sheets and trousers, she'd said to you, *We don't live like this.*

※

GOD TURNS US OVER to what we worship. In the fall, on the Outer Banks, the early afternoon gathering gloom over the ocean in the east is a peculiar darkness, a kind of darkness that

can cast your mind into a wonderful place to express all sorts of
things like ingratitude to God, the failing light perfect for people
prone to such things to commit their sins. Some bad things happen between you and Steve that fall, mainly having to do with
a seventeen-year-old girl. After Labor Day, the people who can
leave the Outer Banks do. The wrecks remain. There are a lot of
burglaries in the cottages around you, and people should suspect
you but don't. A girl punches out all the windows in the nearby
realty office one night after she drinks a quart of vodka alone.
The glass opens her arms from her wrists to her elbows, and the
doctors said the only thing holding the flesh together was all
the bracelets she liked to wear. She is almost bled out, sitting in
the dark in her rocking chair, when you find her. She has called
out weakly to you in greeting as you just happen to walk by from
a depressing evening at the nearly empty dance pavilion. You
could smell all the blood. She had been a popular girl all summer,
and her parents come and get her and take her away to a mental
hospital.

Steve goes out on steel hulls, and you take a couple of trips
on the wooden shrimp boats down in Core Sound. You raft
alongside a local boat one night, a real horn-callused barefoot
fisherman from Wanchese. He's from the old school of Wanchese
fishermen; if you work on their boats, you'll be *singing hymns and
slinging fish*. His wife is with him, two children, a boy and a girl,
all barefoot and sunbaked, all old with a kind of knowledge you
do not possess. They invite you for supper to their galley table
overflowing with cucumbers, fish, fresh biscuits, tomatoes, okra,
corn, and the fisherman thanks God for the plentiful harvest, the

abundance of the water, the blessings of his wife and children, for the fellowship with you. There's a Bible in the wheelhouse for the time between hauling in the nets.

Later that night you have the wheel of the little shrimper, an old one, wheelhouse on the stern. The night is moonless and cloudless under a canopy of stars so dense it makes you claustrophobic, and it's hard to breathe. You're homesick and unwilling to go home; undone by a young girl and beyond broke, you feel bankrupt. The last time you were in the hospital a candy striper kept coming by, a girl probably your age, and you kept wondering why she kept coming around, you weren't encouraging her, and she didn't seem to know why she kept coming around either, but after a while you looked forward to her visits, and on the last day before you went home, she brought you a little blue palm-sized New Testament and you didn't think she was that kind of girl, and maybe she didn't either, because she says, handing it to you, that she felt led to give this to you, and she had written some words in the front cover that you have to this day, and some of the words say, *A friend of mine once said that there were two things in life that last and that is man's soul and God's word. So I thought I'd give you God's word so that you may grow in Him and be whole.* The night at the wheel of the shrimper you know you are steering into a dark that will stay dark for a long time.

ON YOUR LAST TRIP NORTH the captain and the mate shoot up vodka once they finish off the heroin they've brought. A guy tries to knock you overboard one night after arguing about a rain

hat. Your trawler is boarded by the Coast Guard at gunpoint
and forced into Cape May, where everyone decides to go out on
the town, everyone putting on his best wear: black pants, black
T-shirts with motorcycle logos and skulls, wallets chained to
belts, hobnailed boots. The crew popping pills and snapping
open dangerous-looking knives—bucks, martial arts, and the first
stiletto you have ever seen and which you subsequently steal.
About ten of you walk the bad streets adjacent to the docks at
Cape May, a scythe up the street of black and trouble, except for
the one element that is you: slicked-back long greasy hair, scrag-
gly beard, sure, but wearing the only clean clothes you could find
in the bottom of your duffel, the irrelevant college clothes—the
pristine white corduroy slacks, baggy with the weight you've shed
on deck, and the baby blue Izod alligator shirt, tight with new
muscle, purple variety-store flip-flops clopping around your feet.
And still you swagger with the rest of them, looking exactly like
what you are, some assholish seafaring preppy impostor.

The swagger also helps hide the pain, your pelvis is cracking and your femurs are flattening from lifting dredge gear, lifting
eighty-pound wire baskets of scallops and carrying them across
a rolling wet deck, standing for hours as you shuck in the constant movement of heavy weather. The pain is so perfect that it
has a color, its color is silver. You can only sleep because of total
exhaustion, or a draw from a pipe, or a pill from a mayonnaise jar
someone is passing around. Even then, the bone-on-bone silver
perfect pain sends you out-of-body while you are below deck in
your bunk next to the engine room. Sometimes you hover over
the trawler looking down on the other watch working, and one

night, shipping out of Key West, you out-of-bodied back to the island from your at-sea anchorage, and you saw a girl you'd been interested in with another guy wearing a white fedora with a black band around it, and when you got in later and asked her about it, she said it was true.

You are thinking about the girl down on the Outer Banks, the seventeen-year-old, and you slip away from your crewmates to call her from a pay phone, charging the call to your parents' number. It must be two or even four in the morning. You don't realize the operator will call your parents' house to get authorization to bill the call to their number. The operator wakes your parents up, and your father answers the phone and gives his permission, thinking you are calling collect, and then waits for you to come on the line, and you never do. Your mother later says that your father sat at his rolltop desk in the dark for a long time holding the old black receiver to his ear, waiting to hear your voice before finally hanging up and getting back into bed, where she says she could hear him not sleeping until it was time for him to get up and go to work at the paper mill.

ONE DAY A STORM BRINGS YOU HOME to find that they have bulldozed all the shacks around where you and Steve live; the power and water to yours have been cut, but you continue to sleep there. You hot-wire the current and find the water main. The same storm brings Steve home early, and you try some false hilarity for a while: the storm has washed thousands of pounds of green bananas and broken crates up onto the beach. With

the salvaged lumber you two build a new front porch and steps
to your place, placating for a while the guy who owns it when
he finds you squatting. But by Thanksgiving you and Steve go
your separate ways, and by Christmas you are on Marathon Key,
Florida, watching smugglers unload bales of pot one night at a
public dock under the direction of a deputy sheriff. Art and his
best friend, caught up in a disagreement concerning Art sleeping
with the best friend's wife, had let their subchaser sink at a dock
far short of the Caribbean. In your and Art's southernmost mis-
adventures you spend a night in Cuban custody along with other
fishing-boat crews trying to ransom refugees out of Mariel when
Castro temporarily opens the port. Art had refused to take the
convicts the authorities loaded onto your boat; they weren't on
the list of relatives the Miami nationals had given you when you'd
left Marathon Key. It was either relent or remain in jail, and so
you and Art relent, locking yourselves in the wheelhouse on your
return with a .22 rifle and a revolver, keeping a wary eye on the
dozens of prison-pale men who lounged on your decks. In the jail,
you pledge to God that if ever given the chance, you'll go home,
embrace your folks, go back to school. But given the chance,
you'll head for the Outer Banks instead.

First you sell some blood and with the money you buy a bus
ticket, and the bus driver threatens to put you and an underage stripper off at one point when she dances in the aisle, she's
on a drug and you just happen to be sitting next to her, it was
the only seat left, you try to tell the bus driver. You wake up in a
bus-terminal yard and it's dark and you and the underage stripper are the only ones left on the bus. You go into the bus station

and see that you have missed your connection so you wait for hours for the next bus home, drink beer with some bums near a pay phone, and finally, when you get home, the bus lets you off in front of the dry cleaners that is behind the ice-cream parlor where the local nurseryman's eldest son is buying an ice-cream cone with his boyfriend from out of town. They give you a ride to your house. You have to ring the doorbell because you have long since lost your front door key. Your mother opens the door and even though you have not written to her or your father in at least four months and you haven't called either and they've had no idea where you've been or whether you are alive or dead, your mother lets you into the house, you can't read her face, she is a stranger opening the front door. You come in and drop your sea bag in the hall and you come into the living room and then you see that she has set a place for you at the dining room table and she has made your favorite meal. For some reason known only to mothers and to God she has known that today is the day that you will be coming home.

※

STEVE AND A BUDDY HAD SWUNG through Key West on their way back from a dive in the Dry Tortugas at the height of shrimping season, with hundreds of trawlers working out of Stock Island and the Singleton docks. The very first stranger they stopped and asked if he knew you was a guy you'd met from New Bern, North Carolina, who was running a stolen-bicycle operation from a boat he and a cohort were painting, hundreds of bikes stacked in the hold. You'd met the New Bern guy when he'd tried to steal your tandem bicycle, which you'd left unchained in front of Sloppy Joe's. The bicycle thieves were later found murdered in their bunks. You were glad to see Steve, and when you drift north, back down to the Outer Banks, you find him living in a trailer on the canal in Wanchese, his yard littered with busted and ongoing business transactions, surfboards, outboard motors, dead cars, a Harkers Island rig, and a homemade houseboat that was slowly sinking at the dock despite the array of car-battery-powered bilges Steve had rigged to keep it afloat.

SATAN DEMANDS TO SIFT US like sand through his fingers, and God, knowing everything, allows it. You stand on a chair at a table full of friends at a soundside bar not far from Jockey's Ridge, everyone beered and jazzed up on white powder, and you suddenly stand wearing black sunglasses because even at night in your circumstances, light hurts your eyes, and you want an amen from the table, and they give you an amen, and you start a ranting preach about the coming of the Lord in glo-ree. *Jee-zuz be praised*, and your table is laughing and shouting *Tell it!* as you have all seen this firsthand, and you proceed to tell it, you proceed to tell the parable of Jesus At the Carwash, and it begins, *Jesus saw a man, yuh, walking along the highway, yuh*, and you preach the gospel and compare it to the wash, rinse, and wax cycle of a carwash where Jesus is singing hymns and slinging rags on the hoods of cars in the parking lot, and, word of the Lord, you shout out for hallelujahs from the whole place at the end, and the whole place complies, shouting praise and ordering another round, and in the men's room later a man comes up to you and says, *Brother, where do you preach?* and you have to tell him you don't preach, you're not a preacher, you were just messing around, and the man looks at you for a while, he may have come in late and just caught the praises, and he's disappointed at first that you don't preach nearby, and then he realizes the depth of the deception, and he's so disappointed in you that you go out in the parking lot and wait there for the rest of your crowd to finally come out much later.

YOU AND STEVE USE A BOOTH in a restaurant in South Nags Head as an office from which to work your scams, Steve having recently started going out with a waitress there. You have taken on the names of Sven and Sven, dreaming up business ventures over home-style platters and free draft beer: taxis for drunks, boat painting. The people in charge of the boat railway where Steve has hoisted a prison warden's boat, the hull of which he'd been hired to scrape and repaint, notify him that his time has run out, so you run down there and slap anti-fouling paint onto the hull even as the railway owners are sliding the boat back into the water. You apply a wavy waterline from a rowboat.

The warden, a quiet man, comes down to check your progress one day. *Mark and Stephen*, he says; *one was stoned, and the other was a prophet.* At that time you are confused as to which was which. The warden likes you guys until you take his boat out all day when the Spanish mackerel are running, and in the afternoon, when you and Steve come back with hundreds of dollars' worth of fish, there is the warden on the dock with a flock of lost children he is trying to shepherd from errant paths. They'd been waiting for you to return the boat for hours. Those are some terrible faces on those children.

YOU TAKE ONE LAST TRIP with the notorious captain, this time earning the right to step aboard just as his trawler is about to leave the dock. You'd learned enough so that you are actually able to run the winches and read the lorans. With the money, you fulfill your promise to your father and return to your little college in a battered truck and with a beard, wild girlfriend only temporarily in tow. At Christmastime, when you go to her family's house, her sister, the one you should have met, says, having had a lot to drink, that the family is surprised that you are as normal as you are, since most everybody thinks your girlfriend is literally insane. That explains a lot. You take a last writing class with Jim Boatwright, and write about being on a trawler during a storm that rolls the trawler over and the captain has a heart attack and you and the rest of the crew, all teenagers, have to bring the boat back to the dock, the captain nailed into a locker because his body was getting all bruised up rolling around the floor of his cabin, autobiographical. You make two short films violating film school policy that cameras were not to leave the little Virginia town limits. You take the best camera down to Rodanthe on the Outer Banks both times. The first film is about a guy whose insane girlfriend leaves him and he decides not to stalk her. The second is about a lonely plane spotter, binoculars up to an empty sky, living in a tent in the dunes during World War II. One night something crawls out of the surf, disembowels him on the beach, and then slips back beneath the waves. The star of the film is your friend with the melted face. Once, drunk, coming back from a lacrosse game, you two were walking along, and some people in a car were staring at him, and he leaned into their window as they leaned away and said, *I don't care anymore!* Your film professor likes both of your films. You watch them now and realize how empty and bleak and beautiful the seascape was back then, enhanced by the grainy black-and-white film, the foam, the birds, the sand, all shades of grey in the monochromatic winter light.

AFTER GRADUATION FROM COLLEGE, you're living in your truck, driving through the country with a sleeping bag and a Coleman stove. You dig foundations for the world's largest shopping mall in South Carolina. You stay with your Cajun aunt and uncle in Louisiana, where your Uncle James tries to get you on with the union in the pipefitter's apprentice program. Meanwhile, you are working digging irrigation ditches, and one day you go into a convenience store to buy some beer and check out the magazines. There's an *Atlantic Monthly* in the rack, and you are surprised to see that you are a finalist in their American short story contest; the judge is John Updike. Boatwright had entered your trawler story without telling you. You swing the nose of your truck homeward.

YOU RENT A LITTLE HOUSE on the Chesapeake Bay and support yourself taking pictures of houses for a realtor. A publisher sees the *Atlantic Monthly* and sends you a letter asking if you have a novel, so you write a science fiction novel called *The Bug Hunters.* It's about shrimp farming in space on an aquatic planet where a father and a son shoot it out with .38 revolvers and there are Brazilian seafood pirates devoured by large eels. You send it to Boatwright for his opinion, and he sends you a note telling you, *You're wasting your time and your talent.* But you can't think of anything to write, so you read the Russian novelists.

You find a new girlfriend, and your new girlfriend's family has lived on a small island in the Chesapeake Bay since the beginning of time. Her father is a ship captain, and she can tap-dance. The realtor is letting you live in a falling-down house at the end of a partially submerged road, and it's on the grounds of an old Indian summer camp. The place is so haunted that some nights you drive completely around Mobjack Bay to spend the night with your girlfriend or her family.

One night when the girlfriend is looking at the scars across your hips and up and down the sides of your legs, she says she thinks the problem with your hips is a good thing, that without it you'd be an even bigger asshole than you already are.

The realtor drives a canary yellow Eldorado and wears madras shirts and is a good old boy selling waterfront estates to the Germans. He has seen you have a way of talking to the rich people about the history of the places, his properties are one river over from Jamestown and Williamsburg, and you have deeply read the history of the area. *This place dates from 1690, the original part of that farm is that long building they use for the barn now, note the long narrow gun ports through which they pointed their muskets at the Indians.* Once, John Lennon and Yoko Ono come down and look at the place where there's the ghost of the girl who broke her neck on the staircase, but you never see her. When John Lennon and Yoko Ono buy the place, the first thing they do is put salt in the corners of the rooms to keep the ghosts away. Once, you are telling a rich German about the 250-year-old estate, and he cuts you off, saying, *Humff! Ze first thing I do is bulldoze it!* You have to tell him you don't think the Historical Commission is going to let him do that. You go up in the realtor's plane and take pictures for the brochures you are putting together, and the realtor wants to know what you want, how about selling the big estates with him, but you load up your truck and move to Richmond with your new girlfriend, whom you've convinced to go to college.

In Richmond, you work for a con artist selling coupon books, you work at the Capitol stuffing envelopes, your girlfriend gives you a black eye when you accidentally kiss a friend of hers after an Easter parade. After the breakup, you live with your friend David in Washington, D.C., where you run a copy machine for the National Organization for Women and stuff more envelopes for Ralph Nader. You see the police shoot a man at the National Monument in some sort of standoff protest. The *Washington Post* headline reads, "Lone Crusader Against Nuclear Madness Slain by Police." The *Washington Times* says, "Mad Bomber Thwarted." You can't pay your rent, so you camp out at a writers colony for a few weeks and read books by Graham Greene and Malcolm Lowry and write a story based on Art and his best friend's wife.

You drive to Virginia Beach and in the classified ads find a job with a small ad agency writing copy for pizza and brassieres. It's a small shop the owners are running up their noses. One day a guy comes in looking for the owners, and you tell him they've gone "skiing," and you ask him if you can help him. He sits down and says he had an argument with his father, who publishes a small military newspaper, and he just bought the newspaper from his father but has no idea how to do the editorial stuff, the writing, all he knows is sales. You tell him look no further, you are his man.

THE NEWSPAPER SUITS YOU, it's all about the Navy and its ships. On the way out of D.C., you had tried to enlist in the Navy, and they wouldn't have you because of your hips. You even drove to the merchant marine school in Piney Point, Maryland, and they wouldn't have you either. The owner of the newspaper is a big, fearless, boisterous guy with a beard who reminds you of the pioneer in the TV show who lives on the frontier with a pet grizzly bear. His wife, who keeps the books, is a pretty Cuban girl with a nice Tidewater accent. She keeps a sharp edge on her accounting pencil and on her carving knife at home. You know the front office will be secure, and it looks as though you can bank a steady paycheck of ninety dollars a week because money is tight and you don't care, and after all the sales and layout people go home, you and the owner and his wife run the vacuums and mops and brooms and then go have nice dinners at a restaurant that advertises in your newspaper and pays in trade.

Your editorial desk is in a room with a gaggle of salesgirls, some of whom have substance and boyfriend problems. A couple will come back from long lunches disheveled and clammy, and will brag about landing a new account in the backseat at a used-car lot or in a quiet corner of a bed and mattress showroom. The girls are funny and loud, and you like them a lot.

In the back the layout people are generally potheads who share their dope and tell you when good funk bands are coming to town.

Overall it's a good place, and you fill the pages with your name and several of your pseudonyms. You cover the world's largest naval base and its air wings, NATO, the shipyards, the weapons centers, and anything else that interests you, and it all does. You interview admirals and senators, enlisted men, pilots, and junior intelligence officers in their crisp khaki skirts whom you talk into taking you into the restricted areas down in Dam Neck. You write editorials for the Op-Ed page, and you write scathing letters under fake names back to yourself, and you write letters the next week in answer to those, and you feel like Mark Twain, and it's a lot of fun to feel like Mark Twain.

AFTER A FEW MONTHS the circulation increases, your boss and his wife have put the business plan into effect that he had argued with his father about, and the base in enjoying all the coverage you are giving them. Ronald Reagan helps, saying his goal is to have a six-hundred-ship Navy. You get a raise, and your boss trades some ad space to a high-rise on the beach where you can live in a penthouse for free. You have been living in a cheap motel on the Virginia Beach strip with a drummer from the Hilton house band, a tall buff Jewish kid named Kenny. It is a transient kind of place. One night there is a fight upstairs among some redneck construction workers building a hotel next door, and somebody goes out the second-story window and lands on the hood of a car outside your window. The roommate of the girl you found who almost bled out on the Outer Banks works in housekeeping. In the evenings you mix manhattans in a plastic hospital bedside water pitcher that a previous tenant had left and wait for your roommate to come home at 1:00 a.m. because it's no use going to sleep when the band shows up ready to unwind. You catnap until 8:00 a.m. and get in your truck and go to the paper. You are young, and this is possible. Kenny says he remembered seeing you once before at the High on the Hog outdoor music festival wearing just bib overalls, no shirt, and a button on one of your overalls straps that said I SHOULD HAVE STOOD IN BED, and when a mutual friend later introduced you as a possible roommate, Kenny's first thought was *Whoa, it's that retarded dude.*

THE CLOSEST BAR TO YOUR PENTHOUSE is across the street on the beach, the Thunderbird Lounge, and it suits you too. It's an off-season nexus of the strip, a strictly locals place. There's the marine biologist moonlighting as the bartender, the undercover cop with the hash pipe, the magician who picks pockets off season, the pretty registration clerk who sleeps with entire visiting hockey teams, the rubber auto parts satyr, the commercial fisherman who tells you there's a Carolina logger in *Moby Dick*, there's the enormous leonine bookie, there's the owner of a nearby bar whose arms are always broken in casts because he can't pay his gambling debts, the two gay busboys who will later be convicted of murder, the Navy nurse junkie, the tragic widower, the duck-carving hero of Guadalcanal, the mob boss's son trying to become a fireman, the doe-eyed harelip girl who always wants to sleep with you, and there's old Fitz, the driving instructor who has his own shamrock shot glass in a special place behind the bar to steady his nerves after a day riding shotgun with old Filipino women students on the expressway.

There's Witcher, whom you meet the first day you set foot in the place, who entered talking about having approached a single-lane, one-mile bridge over a swampy river hauling a repossessed double-wide house just as a big rig tandem log truck was entering the other end, no possible way for both trucks to pass on the ancient rust-cornered span, but neither seeming to back down, and Witcher saw the log truck and the log truck saw Witcher and they began accelerating toward each other, both blaring their big diesel bassoons, big Witcher working through the gears of his tractor truck, seeing the log truck beginning to furiously flash its headlights but not slow down either, both barreling down to the point of impact in the middle of the bridge, Witcher saying he just kept pouring it on, and you could tell he didn't know why, *he was just led to do it.* You've crossed that bridge many times and had ridden a tugboat beneath it, in fact it's where the tugboat once sank and a steamboat was overturned by a white tornado on a full-moon night years before. Witcher said just before the point of almost head-on impact he flung himself across the seat . . .

It is here in the story Witcher lifts the water glass of vodka to his lips and drinks about half of it and sets it back down, and the bar allows the warm rush of the alcohol to settle his nerves before someone says, *For God's sake, what happened?!*

He says the first thing that happened was that the mirrors on either side of his cab were ripped off: the right side by the girders of the bridge and the left side by the leading edge of an oversized load of loblolly pine logs. The edge of the logs must have then caught the leading edge of the repossessed part of the double-wide home because he felt a shearing feeling and the noise of a great impact as the boarded-up wall to the transported living room was ripped off, its pieces exploding into space and fluttering down into the river, and then there was nothing for a long time, or what seemed like a long time, and he realized the truck was still racing forward, and he didn't know if it was going off the side of the bridge or still barreling down the bridge, so he decided to sit up and get back behind the wheel, so he did, and the truck was flying across the bridge at a great speed *about* to veer and plunge off the bridge, so Witcher grabbed the wheel while sneaking a look in the rearview mirror, where the log truck's brake lights were lit through braked-wheel skidding smoke betraying that the driver had lost his nerve or had become confounded, and Witcher also saw cheap living room furniture, a fold-out couch and an ottoman (you remember his saying *ottoman*) and other crap blown out on the bridge road, and he realized he's lost the inboard and maybe outboard walls to the repossessed double-wide he was hauling, but he had not lost his nerve, had driven what remained of the repossession and delivered it as it

was to the double-wide dealer boasting low, low prices just outside of Suffolk, had gotten in his car and driven straight to the
Thunderbird, and there he stood finishing the bottom half of his
straight water glass of vodka, no ice, a Pepsi chaser.

You will remember the story because you have a reporter's
notebook in your back pocket and because afterward you go in
the bathroom and you write it down sitting on the lid of a toilet,
thinking, *Here I am, I have found a home among some of God's
other special children.*

※

THE SECRETARY AT THE PAPER knew to call the T-bird bar phone
when anyone was looking for you, either there or the putt-putt
golf course down on Pacific. You were usually at either place in
the late afternoon. It's where your mother calls you one night
from a neighbor's house in your hometown. Your father has been
drinking and listening to his jazz records, and she asked him if he
wanted her to put his dinner on a plate, as usual, because he was
doing what he usually did when he came home, opening up the
freezer, putting ice in a glass, and from the stove she would hear
the noise she said she always dreaded, the clink of his flying tiger
class ring tinking against the bottle of bourbon as he grabbed it
from under the sink. Your sister, a teenager now, has told you she
couldn't bring friends home because she wasn't sure what they'd
find. This night, a rainy night, your father has grabbed them both
by their arms and thrown them out the front door into the rain,
slammed the door, loudly locked it, and turned off the front porch
light.

You drain your glass at the T-bird and get in your big green Caprice with the 350 engine, and you burn up the forty-seven miles to your house. You break into your house and grab your father up out of his stuffed chair, where he looks up pleasantly surprised at first to see you, Coltrane blaring, and you grab him by his arm and throw him out the front door, but he's in pretty good shape from working on the lake property, and the time you remember as being almost the last time you see your father will be this time when you're pushing each other around in front of your house in the rain and wrestling down in the mud.

UNDER THE LAW, YOUR father is entitled to anything he has brought into the marriage. When he backs up a truck to your mother's house to claim what is his, you have sent your mother and sister away, and you have two friends there to back you up, one is David, the son of The Preacher, the other is George, a son of the Commonwealth's Attorney. Your father takes the old carved beds and marble-topped dressers and big furniture, dining room table, dressers, plus all the hand-painted vases and china and silver and pretty much anything else of value except a couple of things you have hidden off-site, a clock your grandfather said was yours one day, a .30-.30 Winchester your grandfather used to hunt with in the East Texas bayous, and an aluminum ladder you use to put up Christmas wreaths on the front of the house.

He's angry when he can't find it all. Then he says something you don't understand. He tells you he's hauling your trash. You just shrug and say, *Get your stuff and go*. When the moving crew he has hired, big thug-looking guys who seem to specialize in this type of thing, get impatient toward the end waiting for your father to find the things you've hidden, your father finally comes around to the porch where you're waiting for him to leave. He puts out his hand to shake, and you look at it as if it were a poisonous snake and go in the house.

IT WASN'T EASY BEING YOUR FATHER. A perfectionist with an imperfect child, a son who avoided you, a son who would have preferred to live across the street at the Baptist parsonage. A son who was a stick-figure kid mostly on crutches scared of ice and wet tile.

The good thing about your father being a perfectionist was that he was paralyzed by his perfectionism. Here is a Father Illustration: your father would do all the research on how to do some home repair or home improvement, he would research all the best places to buy the materials he would need, he would buy all the special tools he would need to accomplish the task, and then, afraid of not being able to make the repair, the addition, the improvement perfectly, he would not do any of it at all, so that when he leaves your mother's house, he leaves the garage full of the materials and tools needed to do all the things that have always needed to be done around the house but have never been done by him.

In the months to come, you scrape and caulk, prime and paint while your mother refurnishes the house with things she buys at yard sales and things given to her by friends. She gets a job working midnight shifts as a switchboard operator at the hospital. Your sister needs to look at colleges, so you and friends of the family take her, even though there is no money for tuition. Your mother is not worried, she says God will provide.

THE FURNITURE IN YOUR BEACHFRONT PENTHOUSE is an old broken table, a desk in the living room, a bookcase your grand-father made, and an old four-poster you scavenged from the ex-girlfriend's barn when you lived on the Chesapeake Bay. When your mother and sister come to visit, you have to wheel over a couple of cots you borrow from housekeeping at the Thunder-bird.

At the T-bird Lounge, they play the States Game between Memorial Day and Labor Day. There's a large Rand McNally map pinned behind the bulletin board on the back of the swing-ing door behind the bar. If you get a girl from a state, you get to put one of those little stars like you are awarded in Sunday school for attendance; everybody chooses his own color. At the end of the summer, whoever had the most states wins a prize. Because of Virginia's physical proximity, by midsummer everybody has already gotten Pennsylvania and Ohio. You sit next to a girl and say, *So, where are you from?* and she says, Ohio, and you turn to your buddy next to you and say, *Damn it, I already got Ohio*, and you pick up your drink and move along. On your way home one night you see a friend desperate for Nevada in the front seat of his car, and the buttock flesh and arms pressed against the wind-shield look like a fat man changing clothes in a phone booth.

In spring, there are amphibious assaults on weddings at the country clubs on the back waterways of your beach town, and Witcher has a nice boat, and you all wait until the reception is in full swing before you dock quietly at the end of a private yacht slip. Before the mother of the bride can buttonhole you as to who you are, you've had a drink and dance and have made off with a bridesmaid in Witcher's boat to tie her to your bedposts with the pretty ribbons she's pulled from her hair.

In summer, a girl from New York comes down on weekends, and you're not really sure what she does, she works for a fashion designer, she says, and she packs light, mainly a handful of bathing suits. For you, that summer becomes a big blue star over the state of New York.

Fall is the Whiskey Rodeo. The Navy and the local police want to demonstrate the effects of drinking and driving, so they set up a large municipal parking lot with a twisting course marked by orange cones. They invite the local media to come down and participate. About a half dozen reporters will drink whiskey, wine, or beer over a certain time and then drive their own cars through the obstacle course, all the while the news groups will tape it for a segment. You see the woman who always gets green just riding the helicopters out to the aircraft carriers when the media would go meet a returning battle group. There's the photographer who has volunteered from the daily paper who always had a joint to share before you got on the helicopter. You decide to take your drinks in shots of bourbon. The art department has painted a landing strip on the hood of your car as if it were an aircraft carrier and stenciled the number 69 on the door like the aircraft carrier *Eisenhower*. You said sure they could do it, not thinking they would.

People at the Whiskey Rodeo are crunching orange cones even after one drink. But not you. You have downed five shots and run the course perfectly. *That's the end of the demonstration*, they say. You say one more, so you pour yourself a big shot and down it and announce that you're going to do the course backward. The police make a move to stop you from getting in your car, but you get in, laughing. Of course, you flatten all the orange cones, and a couple of people have to jump out of the way. *Okay, fun's over*, somebody says, and instead, you do a really big doughnut in the parking lot, honking the horn and waving for the one news camera still rolling, and then you leave the parking lot heading south on General Booth Boulevard.

Down the road you realize you're the only one laughing. You look in your rearview, there are no blue lights yet, but probably there will be soon. It's getting dark, so you decide to floor it out to a subdivision that is still being built by a crooked developer who once boasted that he had never read a book in his life. You get out there, and there's a house lit up, and it's a Model Open House somebody has forgotten about and the garage door is open, so you pull in and hit the garage door down. You go in the living room and the kitchen with the fake fruit in the bowl and the stack of flyers and wait, and nothing happens. You go into a bathroom off the laundry room to piss, and there's a water snake in the toilet, or else somebody didn't flush a long, perfectly coiled turd with a head and eyes. It spooks you, and to this day you don't know what it was. When the timers shut down the lights in the Model Home, you creep back to your penthouse, go to the T-bird, and watch the eleven o'clock news with Brian, the marine biologist bartender, and are grateful to see the Whiskey Rodeo didn't make the news.

\\|//

THE PROBLEM WITH ASKING GOD for signs is that He sends them. You drive along a country road late at night and see a little cross atop a little church lit with a spotlight and you say, Okay, if You are real, make that light go out, *and the light goes out*. Shooting stars are too easy, especially on the water. Even that one time you are pissing off a dock in Marathon and you say, I *really* need a sign, and something falls out of the sky so bright you can read a newspaper, and you know you didn't imagine it because your wheelhouse radio bursts alive with chatter: *What the hell was THAT?*

After the Whiskey Rodeo, you are strongly encouraged by the police to make amends. You know what that means. You don't want to be stopped down in the dark part of the county in April by a beach cop with an August attitude and when you roll down the window he says, *I'm thinking of a number between one and ten*, and he's studying his thumbnail, working the little banged-up places on the end of his unsheathed billy club, while his partner watches for any headlights that might come along before they pull you out of the car and adjust your attitude.

So for your sins you are assigned to Crash and Burn. You'll ride with rescue squads who pick up the pieces of the young sailors when the fleet comes in and they take their six months of paychecks and buy overpowered cars and motorcycles. They call the head-trauma wing of the Norfolk hospital the House That Honda Built. You'll ride and report what you see.

At the first accident scene, you can smell the beer in all the blood. It's hard to tell how many guys are in the accordion of car that missed the dogleg turn off Oceana Boulevard and plowed right into the bull's-eye of the hazard sign. They're all dead. You can't look but you do and see a bloody arm coming out of a T-shirt that seems to be coming out of the glove compartment. There are some skin magazines on the folded-up backseat floor, and they look as though they might be gay magazines, but you can't tell and you don't care, it doesn't matter, they're all dead.

The next is in broad daylight. You go to one of those faceless Navy housing ghettos, and there's the young girl hysterical at the front door: *The snake is eating my baby! The snake is eating my baby!* It's the home of one of those asshole guys with the ninja crap on the walls and a boa constrictor or some large snake in a tank, and he leaves on deployment and gives his wife careful instructions on how to feed the goddamned snake, she's supposed to take live mice and dip them in vitamin powder and feed them to the goddamned snake, and she can't do it, who can blame her, and the snake gets hungry and pops itself out of its tank and makes its way over to the crib. The snake gets in there and unhinges its jaw and starts to try to swallow the baby headfirst when the mother comes in from the neighbor's laundry and the baby is screaming with a snake on its head like a skullcap with a length of yellow and brown tail. Nobody knows what to do. One of the EMTs is a woman who tries to calm the woman and almost faints herself, the other EMT holds the snake's neck as if he can squeeze the top of the baby's head out of the snake's mouth. Suddenly you're a Boy Scout, and you take down one of the asshole's ceremonial swords, and you tell the EMT to get out of the way and he does, and you chop off the goddamned snake's head, and the baby is going to be fine except for some small punctures in its scalp after they cut the snake's head off of it, but the worst part is when the snake's body goes off twisting and banging headless into the furniture and knocks over the baby changing table and twists all around it, dying.

What do you want? your boss asks you one night in a strip club. You don't know what you want; you seem to have everything you need—job, girlfriend, car, bar, beach. Historically, as with the realtor, when your employer asks you this question, it's always like a sign from God that you're about to move on.

When your employer springs this question on you, historically you've not been smart enough to ask for a raise, you take the question literally, and you think you might want to live in New York and be a writer, even though you've not really thought this out and you're a little surprised to think it to yourself at that moment.

At that moment outside the strip club you sit in your boss's car, and you haven't said what it is you want yet. While you're thinking, a black man comes out of the strip club dressed all in black leather, you'd noticed him in the strip club, mainly because he wouldn't take off his black motorcycle helmet and they'd asked him to leave. He makes a big show of pulling on his black gloves and getting on his big black motorcycle and kicking it started and loudly revving up the engine, but something engages and the motorcycle gets away from the motorcyclist. Suddenly the black guy is driving his big black motorcycle up onto the hood of some redneck's pristine Trans Am muscle car parked beside him, the motorcyclist putting his front wheel through the redneck's windshield, where it looks permanently stuck. It is one of the most incredible things you have ever seen as the black guy tries to get his motorcycle off the hood of this redneck's car and you and your boss, who has become one of your best friends, are laughing as hard as you will ever laugh in your entire life, and the only thing you want and the one thing you have wanted since is to always be able to laugh that hard again.

YOU KEEP WORKING FOR THE NEWSPAPER and read books by the Thunderbird pool. You read books and play dominoes with Brian and drink pitchers of beer when the bar is slow. The books these days are short books often with a few short stories. Some days you finish a book after just one pitcher and pass the book to Brian, and you begin to think you could write some stories *at least as well* as that.

So you start writing stories about things you know, stolen boats, busted dope deals, petty murders, strange weather, things you see firsthand in the T-bird Lounge. You send them to *Esquire*, sometimes one a week, and they keep coming back. Sometimes they have notes attached suggesting you rewrite the story, but you never do; you toss them in the trash.

An editor at the magazine, Tom, calls you and says he likes

one of your stories, do you want to work on it with him? Nah, you say, you tell him you'll just send him another one, you don't have time to work on the story, you're on deadline for *Ship of the Week*. Okay, he says, he says he's coming down to the Outer Banks that summer, if you get a break, maybe you can get together. Okay, you say.

When you meet Tom, he tries to tell you how things work. He says if you're serious about writing fiction, you should move to New York. Okay, you say.

Finally you read a book of stories you like, and you close the book, and you're facedown on a chaise lounge by the T-bird pool, and you're looking down at the pretty girl on the back cover, and she is looking back, and you get up and walk into the T-bird Lounge and announce, *Boys, I'm moving to New York City to be a writer!*

No one pays any attention to you because you often walk into the T-bird with its dramatically fast-opening pneumatic door with something dramatic or stupid to say. Recently you'd said, *Remember, boys, Abraham Lincoln didn't die in vain, he died in Washington, D.C.*

But they see you quit your newspaper job, which gets you evicted from the penthouse, and you start crashing on their sofas, and Brian the marine biologist bartender's wife wonders for how long when she finds you scavenging their refrigerator one afternoon. Brian says don't microwave anything you find in the freezer, a lot of those are toxic fish specimens. When you mention there's a couple of frozen seagulls in there, he says, yeah, that's another project.

You meet an industrial furniture dealer's mistress at the
T-bird, and she leans on her boyfriend to get you a job working
for some rough guys carrying Makita drill guns and crystal meth
putting together cubicles on military bases on long weekends.
You're valuable to them because you can read blueprints and can
sort the hundreds of crates coming off the trucks for seventy-two
hours without a break.

During a job in Hampton at Fort Monroe you visit the on-site
museum where Jefferson Davis was held after the war, the sun
dappling a pattern on the ceiling of the upper masonry wall of the
cell just as it must have done when Jefferson lay watching it in his
bunk all those months considering the Lost Cause.

Your roommate in the cheap motel the company pays for is
a black guy who drinks gin in the dawn when he thinks you're
asleep. You can hear the tin metal cap spinning off and back on
the gin bottle, the sipping in between. God, he looks familiar. For
a few days you can't place him. He says you look familiar too. He
also says about women, *It all a hole.*

Going out the door one morning, you turn and see him put
on his hat, and you say, *You're one of the Blind Boys, aren't you? I
remember you from the radio days.* He says he thought you looked
familiar when you talked. He says he sometimes used to fill in
when his uncle needed him to. *But I ain't blind*, he says. *I see
that*, you say, and you all go to work.

‧‧‧

IT IS THE WEEK OF YOUR THIRTIETH BIRTHDAY, and instead of
sitting in a wheelchair, you are hitchhiking along Virginia Beach

Boulevard after selling your car. You are moving to New York City to become a writer.

It turns out your New York girlfriend is a swimsuit model who is in videos in store windows on Fifth Avenue. She finds you a place to stay on a futon on a friend's floor in Queens. You call Tom and say, *I'm here, now what?*

You and he sit in a bar, and he draws up a list of ways you could possibly become a writer. One thing he puts on the list is a writing class with a guy who is an editor at a publishing house. The class costs two thousand dollars. Tom is not so sure it's a good fit for you, but you think it's kind of like a lottery: you buy in on the chance the editor sees your work and you get published, so you borrow the money from your girlfriend and sign up for the class.

The teacher is named Gordon and he wears khaki shirts and trousers and a military campaign hat. The classes are six hours long and are in a rich lady's apartment. Sometimes Gordon talks for the whole six hours, and he says things about writing you have never heard, like what makes art is the occult, the arbitrary, the unexampled, the uncanny, the passionate, the intractable, the dire, the dangerous. When you stand up to read a story you've written about a storm at sea, after a couple of sentences he tells you to sit down, that you're just writing adventure stories for teenage boys.

Maybe Tom was right, this isn't a good fit for you, so you go see Gordon and tell him you'd like to drop out of the class, and you'd like your money back. He says, No refunds. Okay, you say, just prorate it, and he says, No refunds.

Two thousand dollars is a lot of money, and you're still look-ing for a job. In your Queens neighborhood is a bar called the

Irish Pony, and even though it's mainly for Irish, you explain to them how the Irish settled the South, and after a while it's okay for you to drink there. The night before St. Patrick's Day you stay in the bar until dawn drinking green beer and doing shots of Irish whiskey. When you head home, it's starting to get light, and you remember you have a ten o'clock job interview. You take a cold shower and put on your cheap grey summer suit and pick up your cheap plastic briefcase and head to the No. 7 train stop. The cold doesn't seem to help sober you up.

When you get into Manhattan, there's a big parade down Fifth Avenue that you have to cross to get to your job interview. The policemen will not let you cross. About a hundred bass drums come down the avenue booming, booming, booming, and the booming feels as if someone is punching you in the gut, and you look around and there's a construction site and you have to stand on tiptoe to throw up green beer and Irish whiskey into a Dumpster. Some construction workers look down and laugh at you and point. You wipe your mouth slime on your suit sleeve and dab at the puke on your tie with a handkerchief, and when there's a break in the parade, you tuck your little plastic briefcase under your arm, and you limp across the avenue the best you can.

Upstairs in an office building you check in with a receptionist who leans away from you when you tell her you're there for your job interview, and you hope you have a breath mint. She tells you to have a seat. The next thing you know two big guys in dark jackets are shaking you awake where you've been curled up asleep in a fetal position on a couch, your little plastic briefcase for a pillow. You think it must be time for your job interview. Instead, they lift you by your elbows and tell you the interview is over as they bum-rush you out of the office of the business for which you are seeking employment, a public relations firm.

※

YOU FIND WORK BARTENDING FOR A RESTAURANT that is hiring people with Southern accents. It's on the West Side Highway. There's a view of the Statue of Liberty across the way.

Things aren't going well for you in the class. You sit on a radiator and glower at Gordon. Two thousand dollars is a lot of money. You decide to write a story for the next class that's a parody of the things the teacher is praising. It's a little story called "Momma Hates Texas." You tell him you've brought something to read, and when you stand up to read, he doesn't stop you, and you read to the end, and he says you've had a breakthrough!

Whether you want to admit it or not, you have had a breakthrough, and Gordon's class is the place you begin to understand what he means when he says an artist can find salvation in his art. You work hard and he pushes you hard, he becomes an advocate for you. He lets you sit in his office and watch him work, he buys you a brandy downstairs when you need one, and gives you a fleece-lined bombardier's hat during one of the coldest winters on record in New York. He will publish your first short story collection, and in his class you will meet the girl you will marry ten years later and who will bear you three sons. You will miss him keenly when later he says you have abandoned him and he has no use for you.

※

THE FIRST PIECE OF WRITING you sell in New York is a true story that happens to you coming home one night from working at the bar. It's about four in the morning, and you're in the bottom of Grand Central waiting for the train back to Queens. You have about two hundred dollars in tips hidden in the storm collar of your old diesel-stained sea coat, the warmest thing you could bring from home to wear in New York City. Three black guys come down the end of the platform, see you, and start to walk toward you. You start walking to the other end of the platform, there's some stairs leading up to a tunnel, but with your legs you know you'll never outrun these guys. When you get to the bottom of the stairs, you turn and there they are, standing around you, and you know what they want. You've never been robbed before. One of the guys reaches out for your arm, and at that moment in the stillness of the station you hear footsteps coming down the tunnel up the stairs. As the footsteps get louder, there's whistling, then singing, a hymn, and you pray to God it's a big Irish cop with a nightstick and a gun, and you see that your three guys hear it and stop and wait to see who it is, and all four of you turn your faces up to the top of the stairs as the footsteps approach and the singing becomes louder.

Suddenly there's nobody there. The footsteps stop, the singing ends, right at the top of the stairs. It seems to be just as spooky for the three guys who are about to rob you as it is for you.

Just then the No. 7 train roars into the station and people get out, including two transit cops, and you get on the train and go home.

The next day you get a call from your mother and she wants

to know how you're doing in New York City. She was against you moving to New York. She says the night before she had woken up wide awake because she had a feeling that you were in danger. She says she got down on her knees beside the bed and she prayed that you would be surrounded by legions of angels.

You write up what happened to you and take it to *Guideposts* magazine, a magazine that publishes stories of faith, the only place you think might be interested. You hand-deliver it, and you notice in the elevator directory that *Playboy* is in the same building, and you remember the bad erotic story you once wrote about a naked woman up a tree at whom enraged townspeople were throwing their shoes.

The editor of *Guideposts* telephones and says to come to the office, where he tells you he's going to run your piece in a section called His Mysterious Ways. He's a pleasant man, and on your way out he says he wants to give you something; he gives you a parallel Bible that has the King James, New International, Living Bible, and Revised Standard versions laid out side by side. Thank you, you tell him, and he smiles and says, *You don't deserve it*.

⁂

YOU GET FIRED FROM THE BARTENDING JOB for stealing a hundred dollars out of the register, even though you didn't do it. It was the slightly autistic bartender you worked with. For three months you and he had been using an old-fashioned cash register, and one night in a crush of people he came up to you and asked you where the Eleven key was on the register, and you tell him it's the Ten and the One keys pushed together, and you realize the source of all the overages and shortages on your shift; you had thought it was just the manager skimming.

FROM THE CLASSIFIEDS IN the *New York Times*, you find a job at a private investigation agency on Wall Street. It's mostly verifying résumés and doing background checks on people handling large sums of money. You're working with a bunch of real New Yorkers. When you all go to lunch and you stand looking up from the base of a World Trade Center tower, they say, *Pretty tall, huh, Gomer?*

Some of the guys working are off-duty cops and detectives, and they teach you how to work the slush pile of cases nobody wants for extra cash, like that of the Korean girl who disappeared in Chinatown, all you have is her last known address. An old cop says to call her landlord and tell her you're the missing girl's boyfriend and you want to come pick up her stuff. The cop gets on an extension and coaches you through it; when you ask the Chinese lady about the girl's stuff, she says, you think, that until somebody pays the back rent, nobody gets the girl's things. The cop puts his hand over the receiver and says you're worried about the stuff, and the Chinese lady says it's all safe in bags in the basement, just bring the back rent, and she hangs up. Good, says the cop, let's go, and he hands you a ConEd hard hat.

You find the address, and when the Chinese lady answers the door, the cop says you're there from the power company. He's got a clipboard, he's told you beforehand that the Chinese are very respectful to people with clipboards and badges. He tells the lady that he's got a few questions for her, while you go in the basement and check the lines. You're nervous, and you go down in a stinking basement and see some black trash bags and go through them, looking for address books, personal items, anything. You find some bank statements, a personal phone book, and a crack pipe, and you stuff them all in your pockets.

Back at the office you spread the items out on the detective's desk, someone else was using the lunchroom table to sift through a bag of somebody else's trash, and by the end of the afternoon you've pieced together that the young girl probably developed a crack habit, went into debt to at least one dealer, maybe two, and they probably did away with her. The cop says there's a catacomb of streets under Chinatown and lots of bodies buried there all the time. Unfortunately for you, you have to call the girl's parents and tell them what you think happened. And since you didn't find the girl, no body fee for you.

Another case is easier. An investment banker was having an affair with his best friend's young daughter out at a country house in Connecticut. When the best friend came home unexpectedly, the banker went out on a second-story ledge that was covered in old snow and ice to hide, naked. While the friend was confronting his daughter about whom she was sleeping with, the guy on the ledge apparently lost his footing and fell to his death on the garden path behind the house, where he lay for a few days until someone found him. The police found footsteps in the snow on either side of the body; someone had come and gone a couple of times, stepping over the body in the snow. You're trying to determine the girl's shoe size because you have a copy of the police report. It was the girl all right, and when she's asked later why she just stepped over the body at least twice coming and going, she said it was because she was *busy, okay?*

You lose your job at the investigation agency because you seem to be unable to master the style of the Account Summation Document. Your reports are too narrative-driven and too objective. In your reports, it's hard to tell if anyone is guilty of anything. One of your buddies tells you the bosses also know that you are writing short stories on company time and they are unhappy that you continue to wear boat shoes to work.

YOU ARE LIVING OUT OF A SUITCASE, carrying a cardboard box of papers and a small electric typewriter from the end of one person's sublet or lease to another. You live up in East Harlem, the only white person in the whole building. There's a jazz bar where you go, and if it's too late to go home, you stay in the bar after the bar is locked up. This is what the owner does for people, lets them stay in the dark at the bar and drink and try to keep track of what they owe. It's in this bar that you meet your cousin. You're holding some Jewish kid by the throat who claims to be a real American because his ancestors came over to Ellis Island in steerage, and you keep saying you had two ancestors who died at the Alamo, goddamn it, and a bouncer is about to throw you out, when the piano player who is on break hears what you're saying about the Alamo and tells you his ancestors' names and you don't believe him, because they're the same as yours. He takes out his wallet and shows you his driver's license; he's named for one of the Alamo heroes.

When a cop gets shot in the face on your block, your cousin

offers to let you stay at his place on the Upper West Side. He
cooks gumbo on Thelonious Monk's birthday every year, and one
night you remember the girl who had just come from her Broadway musical where she stars, and your cousin accompanies her
on his white baby grand, and then an opera singer comes in from
finishing her performance at the Met and sings, and some jazz
players come later, and at some point there are some guys from a
circus, and they are juggling items from your cousin's refrigerator
in a complete circle through the house and over the heads of people, and you have a profoundly erotic experience with a Columbia
coed simply by helping her squeeze the heads off several pounds
of shrimp for the gumbo onto a soggy newspaper in the kitchen.
At daylight savings time every fall, you and your cousin turn your
watches back an hour for every bar you hit until you're drinking
in the distant past.

⁂

YOU GET BY PROOFREADING LEGAL DOCUMENTS at night down
on Wall Street and writing articles for the city's weekly papers,
little impressionistic pieces, like being backstage when Ringling
Brothers Circus comes to Madison Square Garden. When an editor from the *New York Times* calls, no one is more surprised than
you.

The *New York Times* asks you to go down to Atlanta to profile
Jimmy Carter. One thing they don't tell you that you probably
should have known is Jimmy Carter has a contentious relationship with the *New York Times*; and that's probably one reason you
were offered the job.

Mr. Carter is cool to you at first, then loosens up as you meet his wife, and you spend a couple of weeks with them coming and going to the Democratic National Convention, which is in Atlanta that year. At the end of the two weeks, you have an idea of how to put the story together, and Mr. Carter invites you to go to Africa with him, where he's leading a campaign to eradicate river blindness. You call the editor at the *New York Times* and tell her you're going to Africa, and after she hears your pitch that maybe Mr. Carter needed to be president to become the statesman that he is evolving into, she tells you to come back to New York, you're not going to Africa, you're too sympathetic to Mr. Carter. The paper pays you a kill fee, and you're back on the streets again.

It's the first year of the time when the doctors said you would be in a wheelchair, and maybe because you're aware of this, the pain in your hips is getting to you, maybe it's just walking the hard concrete of New York looking for work, often not having subway fare, maybe it's the bitter cold.

You help a guy who has fallen out of his wheelchair on East Seventy-ninth where people keep walking past, and the guy is angry with you for helping as he accepts your help, and all you can say is *I know, I know.*

※

YOU MAKE YOUR WAY TO VIRGINIA BEACH and don't tell anyone at first that you've failed at becoming a writer. You have a canvas cot you found in some trash on a side street in New York, a two-volume edition of *The Oxford English Dictionary*, a suitcase, and your typewriter and box of papers. You hide in a house on the North End of the beach that your old friend Kenny the drummer said was empty, but you are discovered in two days. You see a man on the beach who tells you his daughter has just bought a house a few blocks away.

The daughter lets you stay in the attic apartment of the house she has just bought. Her family is the family that built your hometown. She's beautiful and between her third and fourth husbands and a little lost at sea herself. You insist on paying rent, and she says, Fine, a hundred dollars, and you don't even have a hundred dollars, and she doesn't care.

You've only been gone two years, but there's nobody from the old guard anymore at the T-bird when you wheel a bicycle up there one night and look through the plate glass. You're about to wheel away when you see Melvin. Melvin was with Witcher the day Witcher played chicken on the single-lane bridge, driving his tractor-trailer at the oncoming log truck. When you first moved to New York and were eating beans for the fifth day in a row from a Crock-Pot in Queens, and homesick, you'd called the T-bird one night to tell them that you were coming home. They were having the annual Tacky Tourist party. Melvin had answered and said how proud everyone was of you for going to New York to be a writer, even though New York's a sewer and no place anybody else would want to live, and you'd hung up, realizing you could not go back to Virginia Beach. And yet here you are, and Melvin is surprised to see you. He buys you a drink, and you sit at a table in the corner, and Melvin hears your confession—you don't think you have what it takes to become a writer.

THE NEXT DAY MELVIN TAKES you out in the country in his Jeep and you drive down to North Carolina, where his father was the superintendent of schools, and his mother says it's okay for you to take one of the old mattresses out of the barn for your attic apartment. On the way back to the beach, Melvin stops in a place where he has to collect some rent from some people. You pull in to the yard of an old house up on concrete and brick pillars; there are some dirty children playing in the yard who look up when Melvin drives in as if they've never seen a Jeep with a mattress on the roof before and it frightens them. Melvin says there's a pistol in the glove box, if he's not out in fifteen minutes, to get the pistol out of the glove box and come in the house looking for him.

Melvin goes to the door, and a white woman who's not happy to see him makes a smile on her old face and lets him in.

You watch the children for a while. There are some dogs in the yard, stray-looking mostly. They keep going around to one side of the house and keep sticking their heads up under the foundation, and their throats move as if they are drinking, and you figure there must be a leaking pipe to a tap there, though there is a working well in the yard. You sit and watch for a while, flip down the glove box door, and see the .38 pistol you know there is no way you're going to touch, and you flip the glove box door closed and wait some more.

The door to the house finally opens, and a rough-looking guy lets Melvin out, and Melvin shakes his hand and comes out to the Jeep. You've got one of your little notepads on your lap and you need to borrow a pen, and as you drive off he asks you what you are writing, and you don't answer but what you are writing is: *At night, stray dogs come up underneath our house and lick our leak-ing pipes.*

A friend calls you and says he is one of the judges of a short story contest, and if you send him one, he'll put the fix in for you, it's a thousand-dollar prize. So far you've been eating when the girl in whose house you are staying takes you out to dinner at nice restaurants. Sometimes Melvin comes around and throws pine bark through your open attic window to come out and play, but you are on your mattress in the hot attic going over *At night* . . . because you've learned from Gordon that everything you need is in that first line, all you have to do is unpack the story, its metro-nome is already ticking back and forth.

You finish the story about the stray dogs and send it to *Esquire,* and that's when a new editor calls you up. He's found the story in the slush pile, and they're going to take it and run it, and you hug Melvin and his wife and kiss your landlord friend goodbye and get on a train back to New York.

※

NEW YORK IS BETTER NOW that you will have a story published in a national magazine. You live in a haunted house on East Twenty-second Street that belongs to the girlfriend of a Coast Guard pilot you met at the T-bird one night. Her name is Anstice. Anstice is a caterer, and you eat when you work for her and help her clean out the four-story brownstone, which is pretty much as her parents left it thirty years before. A woman from Barbados who was her mother's nurse still lives there, and the woman from Barbados still talks to the mother, who has been dead for a long time. The woman from Barbados doesn't like the ghost of the

man who walks the top floor and terrifies the bejesus out of you
when you hear him up there.

One night someone leans over you and blows cold breath on
you, and when you tell Anstice, she asks you which bed on which
floor you are sleeping in, and when you tell her, she says, *Oh,
that's just my father coming to see who's sleeping in his old bed.*

When it's time to sell all the old furniture in the place, the
piano movers come to move the piano, and it's the piano Anstice's
parents used to play when they came home late in the evenings
with friends after finishing the shows they'd been performing in
on Broadway. The dead mother doesn't want the piano moved.
At first, the movers can't get in the house; the double front doors
are jammed, even with you inside pulling and the movers outside
pushing. You have to call a locksmith and he can't get the doors to
open; he's taken the locks out and handles off and removed all the
hardware. Then, while you're standing there with the locksmith
and the movers outside, the doors swing open as if they'd been
pushed by a gentle breeze. The movers are spooked, especially
by the running commentary of the woman from Barbados. Then,
when the piano movers are starting to move the piano, the plaster in the ceiling starts cracking and falling in big pieces, and the
movers run outside. Just then Anstice comes out of the hospital
across the street, where she's been visiting a dying friend, and you
call out to her from the window of the room where the plaster is
falling, and Anstice comes in and stands in the center of the room.
She has been crying across the street. Her hands are balled into
fists, her eyes are closed, and she yells, *Mother, stop it!* And it
stops.

When Anstice sells the brownstone, you move into a nightclub kind of performance space in Alphabet City, an old loft where the Communist Party used to print the *Daily Worker*. Where the printing press used to be the old splattered ink is so thick on the walls of the pit they're using as a bar that you can't get paint to stick to it. There's a lot of performance art going on in New York City, and a lot of it gets performed in your new home. There are two levels, six thousand square feet, a first floor with a stage and an upper level with a balcony and a handful of bedrooms around a large common area. You have one of the bedrooms by the grace of one of the guys who had heard you read there and is a voracious reader himself; his family holds the patent on submarine periscopes.

Sometimes you write a story to read onstage. Some of the other acts include a guy who comes out in a tuxedo and sits at a table on which a solitary candle is burning; there's a bucket of water placed on the edge of the stage. Silently, the guy in the chair completely undresses while staring at the flame of the candle. When he is naked, he squats on the chair, still staring at the candle. Then he suddenly leaps over the candle and the table, does a forward-roll somersault, and plunges his head into the bucket of water. People applaud.

There are some nasty comics, two guys and a girl who perform *War and Peace* in fifteen minutes, some guys in blue paint beating drums, and a beautiful girl who performs topless wearing the bottom of a mermaid costume sitting on a stool. She sings "Under the Boardwalk," and when she's finished, she tosses her seaweed hair around and blows kisses. You and the guy whose family holds the submarine periscope patent stand in the balcony and clap until your hands are sore and say, *Now, that's art!*

GORDON OFFERS YOU A BOOK CONTRACT for ten thousand dollars, which is a lot of money for you at the time, and twice as much as he is able to get some of his other writers. You had gone to his office one day to wait for him and there was a letter he was typing to the publisher that was still in the typewriter, and you see your name so you read it. Gordon makes a plea to the publisher for you, saying you are *soul-less* and you blush when you see that, until you read the letter again and realize he has written *sou-less,* without money. When it comes time for you to decide to whom to dedicate your first book, Gordon says *To your mother, Claire, of course.* Gordon does not know that your mother wakes up every morning before dawn so that she can pray for all the people on her prayer list, names of people she has gathered over the years on a stack of worn three-by-five notecards from which she reads and holds during the two hours each morning she prays. He does not know that after you had your breakthrough in his class, his name has been added to Claire's prayer list where it remains to this day.

Your book comes out and nothing happens. A friend of yours who works at the *Washington Post* calls the publicity department of your publisher to get a copy to review, and they tell him you are not one of their authors. When he calls again, they tell him you are dead. You pay off your personal debts and continue to live off the stories you sell to *Esquire*; they end up buying five of them.

The editors there, Will and Rust, often take you to the Broadway Deli for pastrami sandwiches and manhattans. One time at the end of the lunch you carefully pack the uneaten half of your pastrami sandwich, and Rust asks you why you are doing that, and you confess that you're broke again, which is no surprise to Will, who lets you borrow and repay two hundred dollars at least twice a month. Over lunch you have been telling them about the summer previous when you were in Virginia Beach and spent an afternoon sitting on your bicycle watching the police retrieve a body that had been sucked into a sand dredge in Rudee Inlet. You were thinking of writing a story called "Where Blue Is Blue," but you didn't have it all worked out yet.

At the end of the lunch Rust tells you to come by the office the next day, and when you walk eighty blocks on your hips, you find that he's not there, he's just left an envelope with a note. You open the envelope, and there's a note that says the magazine's writers do not walk around hungry, and there's a voucher for an advance against a story he's commissioning called "Where Blue Is Blue." You go home and write the story.

When it comes time for your book to go into paperback, the publisher says it may not be going into paperback. The publisher's office says nobody has been buying your book.

A week later, it's announced that your book has won the PEN/Hemingway Foundation Award and you'll be flying to Boston to receive the award from Norman Mailer.

In Boston, you meet Mr. Mailer and the head judge for the award, Josephine Humphreys, and you're allowed to bring some family and friends, and you fly up your sister and your mother. In your speech you recount your mother bringing you books by the grocery bagful from the library when you were recovering from hip surgery. The ceremony is at the Kennedy Library, and you don't know it at the time, but Mrs. Onassis is in the audience, and when the speech is over and it's time for the dinner, she asks that you sit beside her.

Mrs. Onassis asks you a lot of questions about yourself, and you talk about the ocean and sailing, and she says how much she loves those things, and she says her happiest times were always on a boat, and she says especially that one out there, and you see through the window she's meaning the little sailboat that's on display at the museum. Your mother can't believe she's met Jackie Kennedy, and when it's over, you think it's over, but it's not. In a couple of days one of your roommates at the nightclub performance space tells you he's been hanging up on someone who keeps claiming to be Mrs. Onassis when she calls. He says once when she identified herself, he said, *Right, and I'm the king of Spain!* and hung up.

Mrs. Onassis sends you to her brother-in-law's orthopedic surgeon at the Hospital for Special Surgery. You thank her, but you'll never go. Just recently you had appendicitis, and when, by the grace of a book-loving physician named Bruce Yaffe, you were admitted, the hospital released you early because you didn't have insurance. But soon, the orthopedic surgeon's office is calling to schedule an appointment, and the woman calls every day until you set the appointment and promise to show up.

You see several doctors at the hospital, and they all ask you the same thing: How do you get around? You think they are asking which subway do you take, the No. 6 train? Which crosstown bus? You tell them it depends on where you're going, you suppose. They become a little impatient. No, where's your walker, your wheelchair, your crutches, your cane? They show you your

X-rays—it's all bone grinding into cracked bone. They say it's a wonder you can walk at all. Yeah, I can walk, you say.

Even in the coldest winter a walk across midtown Manhattan has you in a sweat. The doctors are telling you that there is much surgery in your future, but you're embarrassed to tell them that you have no insurance. Thanks, but you'll push on. You call the doctors' office and worry about the bill, but the bills never come. Mrs. Onassis has taken care of them.

In a Sunday afternoon talk with Mrs. Onassis you tell her about the migratory fowl flyways through the Great Dismal Swamp, and she is very interested. You make some calls about when the best time is to take a guided tour, winter probably, or early spring before the bugs and snakes are out. Before you can show her the Great Dismal Swamp, you find out that she has taken ill and has died, though you feel as if you just saw her. One morning you went up to your new publisher's offices, and her office was near that of your new editor, Nan Talese, and on your way out you were lurching up the hall with Mrs. Onassis on one arm and Nan Talese on the other, and people were sticking their heads out of their offices to see what was laughing and lurching so loud going by, and it was just a very happy you.

※

IT TAKES YOU FOREVER to write your next book, a novel. You had once asked Gordon what the hardest thing is to write about. Without looking up, he had said the hardest thing to write about is the love one man has for another without it being homoerotic. The only thing you could think of that would approximate that in your life would be the feelings you once felt for two sea captains on whose boats you had once shipped.

You are lost at sea in New York City, headphones on, Bible tract in your back pocket, the seafaring novel roaring in your head, the heaving concrete, headlong black foaming ocean, a pitched deck where men hold on for life in the shadows, a Master somewhere on the upper deck, unseen but seeing, seeing you, no urgency, no destination, no end to the night, you sail under reefed sail, a stranger pulls you by your collar from stepping in front of an express bus on Fifty-seventh Street.

So you rent a beach cottage down on the deserted end of Virginia Beach in winter to finish the novel, and immediately a nor'easter rips off the front of the house and floods the first floor. You send the girl you've brought with you back to New York while you stay in the ruins of the place. Melvin comes by and finds you with a shovel and a broom trying to clear your driveway, which the persistent winter wind will cover again overnight. Every day you wake up and shovel and sweep until dark and spend every night at the only bar at that end of the beach where you drink until the bartender drives you home at closing, even though your car is in the parking lot and it's only two blocks.

The only other people living in your neighborhood of summer rentals are a pretty woman across the street and her three small children. Her husband is a Navy carrier pilot on deployment in the Med. He's secreted his family here while he's away because someone has been stalking his wife. You eat when she brings you over plates of food or when Melvin and his wife feed you. At Christmas you buy the lady and her kids across the street a Christmas tree, but you won't take it in her house. It wouldn't look right. Once she has a prowler, and she calls you, and you take a pistol over there in the middle of the night and find footprints under a back bedroom window; it could have been teenagers or a hobo. You tell her it's okay, but you sit up on your porch wrapped in a blanket with a bottle in the dark and keep watch until you fall asleep.

When the husband comes home and his wife tells him you kept an eye on them and wouldn't come into the house because it wouldn't look right, he decides he wants to drink a bottle of bourbon with you and you do, and later, when you need a car to drive on book tour, he gives you his 1972 Cadillac Sedan DeVille, gold with brown leather interior, pristine, rebuilt stock-car engine, and a Navy five-shot Smith & Wesson revolver to keep in the seat pocket just in case.

\\///

ON YOUR WAY BACK TO NEW YORK to turn in your novel, you stop by your mother's house. You have Tom Waits's album *Rain Dogs* blaring on a boombox as you sprawl on a mattress on a cheap frame after your father looted the house, and as your mother passes the door, she says, *No wonder you're depressed, listening to THAT*.

You ask *Esquire* to let you profile Waits and ask him about his creative process; there is something in his music that calms you even in its most discordant melodies. You do research into music therapy for autistic children, finding that some music reorganizes autistic children's brain waves. You are also interested in how you can create tension in texts between what meanings the words are conveying on the page and what the sounds of the words themselves are evoking in a reader. Why are certain melodies sad? Melodies without words. You find a theory it all has to do with sound recognition in the most primitive part of our brains and the primal caterwauling of mothers calling their children back into the cave, back into the safety of the fire, the sounds and tones when the children are in sight, nearby but out of sight in the jungle, and, finally, sadly, the grief of when the children having been in the jungle all day and now night is falling, the sound the mother makes when the children are not returning.

You travel to Europe to find Waits, who's putting up a show called *The Black Rider* with William Burroughs and Robert Wilson, both of whom you interview, one is a creep and the other is a genius. You spend two weeks in Hamburg, where the show is a hit, and you see *The Black Rider* several times, and you see snow fall in flakes the largest you've ever seen, the size of silver dollars. You follow the show around Europe, but Waits is not available; someone says you should look for him on the Reeperbahn. You stumble around the Reeperbahn and see the prostitutes in the windows, but you're fearful of all the ice, and you lose your scarf often in the street. You start drinking with the cast and orchestra after the shows and hang out with Robert Wilson but no Waits.

You follow the show to other cities until you are in a small German city somewhere, a grim grey place in winter. A man is demonstrating a carpet cleaner outside of a department store. He has a broom, a donkey, and a crate of carpet cleaner. He lets the donkey shit on a piece of carpet, then he applies the carpet cleaner and sweeps it off, revealing a dirty piece of carpet. You enter one of those deep, deep dark moods, and you stop going to the show, and you hole up in your hotel. There's nothing but fuel-truck racing on the television. It's winter and it's snowing and you're in deepest, darkest Germany.

One Sunday morning it's snowing hard again, and you pack your little suitcase and go down to the train station where it's just you and the ticket agent. You make a promise to yourself that you will get on the first train that comes into the station and ride it to wherever it is going until dark, and you do.

When the train comes into the station, you are the only new passenger, and you sit in an empty car staring out at the fog and snow, and by mid-morning you feel as if the train is climbing but can't really tell because of the dense fog; you hate to do it, but you ask God for a sign. You somehow feel as if you've done your part, by making the pact to get on the first train that arrived in the station, and you have no idea where you're going.

What a comedian God is! The light begins to change, there is in fact light through the fog, patchy light at first, and you lean close to the window in eager expectation. Nothing, nothing, and then suddenly the train bursts through the tops of the clouds, and you see a jagged brown finger of snow-tipped rock any third grader who has seen *You Only Live Twice* would recognize as the Alps. A conductor comes through to take your ticket, and you ask if those are the Alps, and he says, Yah, and you forget to ask him where the train is heading because the mountains are staggeringly beautiful in a transfiguring glare of sun on glacial ice.

That night in the Milan train station some kids try to steal the tiny portable typewriter that one of Robert Wilson's assistants has given you, one that runs on European current, and in the morning you take the first train out of the station going anywhere, and at dark you find yourself in Florence. You disembark and stumble into the nearest four-star hotel, Hotel Diplomat, and you spend a week in Florence, mainly in the Galleria Palatina and the Brancacci Chapel.

It is winter, and there aren't many other tourists. You go back so often to the Brancacci Chapel that a woman who works there selling tickets scowls at you when you keep showing up to stay for hours, and you can't help it. Saint Peter resurrecting the boy who was dead for fourteen years, the cripples cured by his passing shadow, the looks on the faces of the neophytes after their baptism, meditative, confounded, stupefied.

On the Ponte Vecchio you buy tortoise-shell earrings for your agent in New York. At rush hour there are flocks of girls passing on scooters, their skirts snapping in cheeky flourish. When you can't feel good about *Esquire* paying for the four-star hotel any longer, you go to the train station for the first train out, and you arrive in Livorno. In the morning you go into a travel office and ask what's leaving next, and they say a ferry is boarding to Corsica, so you go down to the docks and are swept up with a group of Arabs and arrested by the police.

Even though your hair is shaggy and you are Cajun dark and have a rough beard, the police soon realize that you are not with the Arabs who are holding suspicious passports. When the police captain asks you in Italian what your business is, you try to tell him you are a writer, and the policemen all laugh. While the policemen are laughing, the Arabs make a run for it through a yard of cargo containers, and the police captain smiles and hands you back your passport and says, *Good luck, signora.* It is on the ferry, where people are throwing up over the side because the crossing to Corsica is rough in winter, that you look through your little Italian pocket dictionary and realize you had pronounced yourself a *romanziera*, a lady novelist.

You stay in a hotel in Bastia where the people are also suspicious of you, and in the morning you take the first bus out of town that takes you to Calvi on the other side of the island. In Calvi it is the off-season, and you stay in an old hotel where you are the only guest and the woman from whom you have to ask for extra blankets has tears tattooed at the corners of her eyes.

The hotel is across the street from the fire station, and the firefighters are on strike, so in the evenings they build big bonfires in front of the fire station that the winds whip up as they stand around and drink all night, putting more and more firewood on the fires. You stay for a couple of weeks in Calvi, long enough that everyone from the waiters in the restaurants to the pharmacist from whom you've had to buy flu remedies refers to you as the American. You tour the Genoese castles and discover the place that overlooks the spot where Admiral Nelson lost his eye in the bombardment of the city. The constant drizzling rain that pours down on you in the evenings as you walk the empty streets is not rain; it is the sea spray from waves pounding the ninety-foot cliffs nearby that sound at night like distant thunder.

On the morning you are evicted because it doesn't make

sense for the lady with tattooed eyes and her angry husband to keep the hotel open for one guest, you take a shuttle that is leaving town, and it takes you to an airport, a surprise, and the first flight out is a short hop to Marseille, so you buy a ticket and board the plane.

In Marseille, you buy a stiletto that you lose on the bullet train to Paris. You realize you are returning home as you cross the sea and land, so you let the trains take you from Marseille to Paris to London, where you crash on the sofa of a friend who, like Steve later, will suggest you spend a week, you're looking that kind of rough, and you do, and you think to call *Esquire,* and the first thing they want to know is where in the hell have you been.

You have been traveling on *Esquire*'s expense account for a couple of months now, and it's hard to explain where you have been, and even harder still to admit that you never interviewed Tom Waits. You tell them that you are in London and your only plans so far are to find where Captain John Smith is buried, you've heard it's around the Old Bailey somewhere, it's something you've always wanted to do.

The only thing that saves you is that your seafaring novel is finally coming out, and people are talking about it, and the editors at *Esquire* have said the pretty girl whose stories you loved wants to contribute your first review, can you find a photographer in London to take your picture for the article? So you call a friend and end up having your picture taken by an actress who has starred in nude films and was a girlfriend of Prince Andrew's. You hobble to her apartment because London is hard on your hips, the steps, the cobblestone streets, the cold fog. The door is answered by a young woman in a kimono who has no front teeth and has a perfectly round wound in her forehead like a Cyclops who has had its eye sealed with plastic surgery. She had been hit by a cab and had fallen facedown on her lens cap. You spend a great afternoon with her having your picture taken. She suggests fire cupping on your perineum to alleviate your hip pain, which is no longer silver, more like grey lead. When you see her next in New York, she is beautiful again.

※

ENTERING THE LINCOLN TUNNEL driving out of New York on your book tour, you ask God for a sign. God, never willing to disappoint, provides this: as you exit the Lincoln Tunnel, you see a car stranded in the median, and it is a fireball burning as hot as is possible for a vehicle to burn prior to the flames igniting the gas tank for an apocalyptic explosion. You pull over and take pictures with a disposable camera.

At the end of the twenty-eight-city book tour you find yourself at your friend Steve's house in Pensacola with a dog you have taken out of the highway, and you have uncontrollable shaking in your hands that even shots of schnapps in the morning don't seem to diminish. Your friend Steve suggests you stay with him for a while, and after a week of deep-sea fishing in the Gulf on Steve's boat and sleeping twelve hours a day, you are okay to drive back to New York City. You set out in search of an audience for your book, and you return with mixed reviews and a dog who is half beagle and half rottweiler.

TOM WAITS CALLS.

He's in California mixing *The Black Rider*, he's sorry for the confusion, would you like to come out and do the interview now? You get on the first plane to Los Angeles.

You call an old friend who lives in Venice and ask her if you can flop on her sofa. It's a red-haired girl who was in your writing class, and you always liked her drugged-out surfer-trash California stories. You had a strange thought one time when you were looking at her shuffle her papers on the floor of a rich lady's apartment; you wondered what it would be like to be married to her. People were always whispering that she had a famous father, and when you ask someone who her father is, you have never heard of him. He was a football coach, you don't watch football. When you signed your book to her, you said, *As if you need another brother*, because she already had three older brothers, and that is one reason you always liked her, she had grown up among men, and you felt as if she didn't hold it against you that you were a man. You double-dated with her and her boyfriend, and when she and her boyfriend broke up, you took the boyfriend up to a bar in Harlem where your Alamo cousin Joe was playing the piano. You bought the boyfriend a lot of drinks and told him what a great girl she was and it would be a shame to let such a great girl go.

The interview with Waits is a sit-down at a small Italian restaurant, and you think it will be the first step on a wild night in the gutter with Tom Waits, but it is not. He is sober and polite, gives you some good quotes about the *Black Rider* album he's mixing, and before you can even begin to ask him about his creative process, you can tell the interview is over. When you ask him if you can come into the studio with him, he politely demurs, saying, *Oh, no, it would be like watching someone bathe.*

In the morning you are packing up to go back to New York City, and the phone rings at the red-haired girl's house in Venice. It's Waits, he says it's okay if you want to come down to the studio after all, so for the next four weeks you go into the studio with him at midnight to sit in on the mixing of *The Black Rider.*

During the day the red-haired girl takes you to the beach, which feels good on your hips, and you hang out together on the Strand. This is the girl whom you used to call at two or three or four in the morning when she was in New York and ask her what she was doing, and she'd say, *Sleeping,* but she'd stay on the phone while you recounted the date you'd just had. This was a person to whom you could tell everything, and you did, and now you realize that she's still your friend even after everything you had told her about yourself.

One morning you are lying on the extra bed on the sunporch, where she's been letting you stay, and you can see her through the open door in her office wearing a pair of her father's old pajamas, with her feet up, drinking coffee and smoking a cigarette, reading the sports page, and you think, *Her.*

At breakfast you say why don't the two of you just go down to city hall and get the paperwork done and get married right away. Maybe have some kids. Three. Two boys and a girl.

Her brother is running for governor of your state. The polls show him behind by thirty-three points. When she says she's going to help with his campaign, you volunteer to drive her around the state in your Cadillac handing out campaign flyers and stapling posters to road signs. It's a rainy fall in your state. Often you two are at late-night shift changes in front of factories and shipyards handing out her brother's soggy campaign literature. A lot of the workers are about to ball up the paper and throw it on the ground until they see that she's the daughter of that football coach. All of a sudden she's standing in the rain with these workers talking about the glory days of the Washington Redskins. A couple of the guys always ask her to sign a campaign brochure. It is a long rainy campaign, and you seem to be changing out of wet clothes in adjoining rooms a lot.

Her brother wins the election, she goes back to California, and you drive the coast road back to New York. There is a letter waiting for you there, asking if you would like to teach at a school on a mountaintop in Tennessee that has a fifty-foot cross overlooking a big green valley beyond.

IT'S A SUNDAY AFTERNOON in late winter on the Tennessee mountaintop where there is that fifty-foot cross, and you're alone deep in the woods when you get the call to ministry. All that is needed to round out this greeting-card epiphany would be for your face to be turned toward the bloody setting sun and you saying, *Yes, Lord, yes, Lord, take me, I am yours.*

Instead, you are not watching the sun at all, which is a mistake, because in this part of the world the sun sets quickly over the mountains and you are alone deep down a dark tree alley of an old logging road on the thousands of acres of mountaintop, and it will be pitch-black dark soon, and it is still winter and the temperature will drop below freezing, and no one knows where you are, and there is only your dog at home who would miss you if you do not return.

You have been filling your coat pockets with fossils you find in the muddy banks of the logging road that have been split open by the ice you are still fearful of walking on, and that is how you first saw the fossils, palm-sized reddish orange sandstone pieces with perfect impressions of calamite leaves and branches of lepidodendron trees. Three hundred million years ago these were hundred-foot Dr. Seuss–type trees with cartoon bamboo bark trunks topped with bursts of long thin leaves from the time when the mountaintop was a swampy forest on the edge of a warm shallow ocean.

You are running your thumb over a little twig of a perfect sprout forever part of the stone in the failing bloody light when you feel the Call.

The sun catches you out, and it's a long walk home slipping and sometimes falling where you can't see in the dark, you can only find your way by looking up and seeing what's left of the sky between the wall of trees on either side. *Okay, You have my attention*, you say. Something is changing, and you will never ask God for a sign again.

＊

YOU DON'T TELL ANYONE about this thing that has been placed on your heart. You don't tell Jennifer, the red-haired girl in

California, who is coming out to see you soon, you don't tell the poet at the university, you don't tell anyone; you go about teaching your writing class in your black academic gown on the Cambridge-style campus, and when you sit in chapel during the week, you think about what has happened to you, and you start praying your ass off.

It is good that Jennifer is coming to see you; you have missed her terribly. Your dog loves her, a good sign. She is concerned on a night when she sees you sitting next to a roaring fire you have built in the fireplace and you are sitting so close your clothes are hot to the touch because you need the heat to work on your bones; this is a cold and damp place in winter, and sometimes at the end of the day the pain is making your eyes water, and the fire seems to help.

You noticed when you were at her house in Venice that she burned votive candles to Saint Monica and she threw the *I Ching*. Visiting the mission in Santa Barbara, you find out she has never been baptized. You take her to chapel, and she sees you struggling with something spiritual, and she tells you one day she would like to learn more about faith. At that time catechism classes are starting on the campus for those wishing to be baptized later by the bishop, and you suggest she go to the classes, and she says she'll go if you go with her, and you do.

Just before the Civil War some Episcopal clergy in the High Church tradition trekked up this mountain in eastern Tennessee and founded this college that Union soldiers subsequently dynamited into pieces that they carried home as trinkets and heirlooms. The event was depicted in the stained glass of All

Saints Chapel when the church was rebuilt after the war. This is a good place to answer the Call. You begin to make little trips to the admissions office of the seminary on campus, and you quietly pick up some materials. One of your next-door neighbors is a middle-aged man with a wife and kids, and you look for him going out to his mailbox so you can "run into him" out there and float him a few questions.

The bishop is coming at Easter, those wishing to be baptized can do so at Easter vigil the night before, you tell Jennifer this is perfect timing for her. She says, Maybe later. You say, Now. Someone will need to present her as a candidate for baptism, and you tell her that you will do it. You have volunteered to read lessons from the Bible, and this time, because it is Easter and the bishop is coming, there will be a full choir and much pageantry and, of course, rehearsal. It is during a rehearsal that this thing happens to you.

You are sitting in a folding chair with your bit of the Old Testament to read in your hand, and a visiting Anglican bishop from the U.K. pulls up a chair and sits beside you. You have seen him around campus. It is a small college, and he has seen you as well. He has heard you are interested in entering the seminary, and this surprises you, but things like this happen at a place like this and you are the type of person that these types of things happen to. Yes, you are interested. Why? he asks, and you have a hard time articulating that you feel you have heard the Call. And do you know what is going to happen to you here? he asks, and you say you've been reading the catalog for the seminary, it looks good—theology, philosophy, literature, music . . . Yes, he says, three years of all that. Now, do you know what will happen to you once you leave here? Well . . . and you really don't have an answer, but he does. He says, They're going to farm you out to some little Podunk parish in Alabama, and over the course of your life you'll reach maybe a hundred and fifty people. Okay, you say. Look, he says, you're the writer in residence here, right? Yes, the Tennessee Williams fellow, you say. So you're a pretty good writer? he asks, and you shrug, and he says, If you have the Call and you're a good writer, you need to keep writing, you'll reach many more people that way than if you go through seminary.

You can't say that a weight lifts off of you or that a beam of light suddenly breaks through the stained glass and shatters something inside you. It is more like a knowing, like when you're navigating a river upstream during a drought, it's easier to navigate when you know to avoid the tributaries and stay to the main channel.

When Jennifer gets baptized, she has tears in her eyes when she leans over for the bishop to pour water from the baptismal font over her pretty red hair. Still emotional back in the pew, she accidentally sets her Book of Common Prayer on fire with her candle. A couple of weeks later she gets a letter from the Episcopal Diocese of East Tennessee. She reads it and says, *Oh my God, look at this*. It's a certificate certifying her baptism, and it certifies that according to the ordinance of our Lord Jesus Christ, she was administered the sacrament of Holy Baptism with water in the name of the Father, Son, and of the Holy Spirit, and because you sponsored her, you are now her Godfather, she is now your Godchild. You find this exciting in a spiritual and a non-spiritual way.

When she goes back to California to work on her book about

her father, you call the wife of her brother and tell her you would like to know the governor's schedule in the coming months, as you will be needing to meet with him in order to ask for his sister's hand in marriage.

YOUR FELLOWSHIP IS FINISHED. A Mississippi writer named Barry whose work you've always admired calls. He wants to know if you would be interested in teaching at Ole Miss. You drive down to Oxford, Mississippi. Your house is across the street from Rowan Oak, William Faulkner's house. At night you walk your dog over there and look in the windows, but you never see a ghost. The banging against the window from the inside late one night was just the radiators coming on, and you leaped back, and your dog ran all the way ahead of you home.

It is a good town, a welcoming place where two of your favorite writers live. You leave the back door unlocked because you are in the South and people are always coming in without knocking, and that's how you meet Larry, another Mississippi writer you admire, one night when you come in the kitchen and he's sitting there smoking with a bottle of bourbon on the table and he says, *Hey*.

Barry and his wife, Susan, take you and your fiancée out to dinner and have you over to their house for Easter dinner. One of your favorite writings of Barry's is the introduction to a pocketbook edition of the book of Mark, which includes a poem that you have taped to the wall of your office. Jennifer taught with Barry back in Bennington, and he is fond of her; when he hears you two are getting married, he sends a note to her reporting that he is crestfallen with the news, having always envisioned spending his later years as an old man watching the sunset from a condo balcony in Palm Springs while she combed Grecian Formula through his hair. He says he imagined he would be wearing a lot of turquoise.

You and your Godchild get married in California. During the wedding reception, Melvin presents you with a metal pot and a large metal spoon on the dance floor. Melvin is mindful of the time that he and his wife had gone with you and a blind date who you never saw again down to a biker bar to hear some live music and during a protracted drum solo you had gone into the attached restaurant kitchen serving fried fish and she-crab soup and had taken down a pot and a large cooking spoon and returned onstage to the biker bar and yelled *Conga line!* into an open mike and had led several tables of bikers and biker chicks conga-lining through the place. Melvin says it was one of the bravest things he had ever seen, its audacity the only thing keeping you all from getting shot, cut, or killed. You end your wedding reception banging on the pot with the spoon, conga-lining on a terrace overlooking the Pacific Ocean, leading your new wife and all of her friends and family and all of your best friends from all over the world, many of whom do not know each other, though later at a restaurant after the reception, standing and telling how they met you, for most, they met you in a bar.

Back in Mississippi, you start locking the back door, having just come back from your honeymoon, where you, after drinking an entire pot of coffee and taking some pain pills, hiked five miles

across the floor of a volcano's crater. You finish consummating
your marriage in every room of the house, including the backseat
of the Cadillac parked in your very own carport.

⁂

THERE'S STILL THIS MATTER OF THE CALL on your heart.
You attend the Catholic church wondering if Walker Percy was
right about the Church being the true church. You try to talk to
the priest about personal ministries, but maybe you spook him,
because he acts as if you are trying to sell him something he doesn't
want to buy. You've never read Kierkegaard, and now you do, and
you'd like to talk to someone about despair, is it really a sin, and you
go to the Episcopal church, but the priest there one Sunday says
Dr. Seuss is one of his favorite writers, and he preaches a sermon
while turning the pages of a Dr. Seuss book, and you don't go back.

When your time is up in Mississippi, you are sad to go.
You and your dog drive across the country to meet your wife in
California, where she has gone ahead to find you a place for you
all to live while she finishes her book. In Albuquerque you sneak
your dog into a Holiday Inn Express, and in the morning two
policemen are knocking on your door and wanting to talk to you.
During the night, someone broke into every car in the parking lot
except yours, they suspect a Mexican gang, but they're curious
about you. You don't know what to tell them, but in your heart
you're sure it has something to do with the Texas tags and the
Saint Christopher statue glued to the dashboard.

⁂

YOU AND YOUR NEW WIFE RENT A COTTAGE on the old Vanderlip Estate, begun in the 1920s as the Hamptons of the West.
Your cottage is a one-room studio with no heat, set amidst the
overgrown gardens of the mansion, the Villa Narcissa. Teenage
gang members from San Pedro jump the walls at night and roam
the property to see the ghosts, particularly that of the Vanderlip
daughter locked in a private asylum there after an illicit affair with
a black man, and the glowing dogs. There is an old casino on the
property, casitas, stables, and a gamekeeper's house. There are
scorpions and rattlesnakes, abundant peacocks, and hundreds
of cypress-lined steps leading to a temple with an otherworldly
view of the Pacific Ocean and Catalina Island. Elin Vanderlip, the
grande dame, tells you of the many people who have visited since
the 1930s, the actors, the heads of state, the writers, of whom you
are just one.

You write a novel about an orphan who is raised by a reli-
gious prophet, and the orphan turns to a life of crime, becoming
a counterfeiter and switching identities with a black-sheep scion
of a faded-money family, and narrowly escapes being murdered
by a crooked family lawyer dressed in a Santa Claus costume.
Nan Talese calls you and tells you it's gorgeous, beautiful writing,
and she has absolutely no idea what is going on in the book, and,
come to think of it, neither do you.

You go to Louisiana for Uncle James's funeral, and while
you're there, you see five shirtless crew-cut boys who look a lot
like you did when you were their age, you watch them climb up
on a picnic table and jump off over and over and over and over

again and you think, *We should have children*, and when you get home, you find Jennifer skinny-dipping in her mother's pool, and she gets out and stretches on a towel in the sun and tells you she's pregnant.

So your wife is pregnant and you're broke and your novel is a disaster. You take your first edition of Mark Twain's *Connecticut Yankee in King Arthur's Court* and a rare print of Stonewall Jackson's last meeting with Robert E. Lee into Santa Monica to sell, and you run into one of the students who had been studying with Barry at Ole Miss. She's Robert Altman's script supervisor and Altman has told her to write a script for him and she's stuck. So you help her break a movie she calls *Cookie's Fortune*, and she says she can't pay you or give you credit, but she can introduce you to Altman, and that's good enough for you, and you meet Altman, and one of his readers has put one of your short stories in his hands to read, and he thinks it would make a good movie— ensemble cast, strong female leads—would you be interested in adapting it for him? So you adapt your story in about two weeks, and he reads it and says it's good, it'll be his next movie, and you think, That wasn't so hard.

Except Altman always has several next movies, and through the grace of Ron Carlson you are offered a teaching job at Arizona State. It's a big campus and hot, and one day as you are walking across, you realize you can't walk. You have to sit down and it's 113 degrees and you can't move. Despite the white Arizona sun, all you can see is the color of your pain, and the color of your pain is black.

The time has come to amputate the femoral head of your left

hip, hammer in a titanium spike with a Teflon ball, rebuild the pelvic cup, sew you up, send you home. You interview several orthopedic surgeons and you learn that surgeons do not like to be interviewed. The best people who can tell you about a surgeon's handiwork are anesthesiologists and surgical nurses, but they are reluctant to talk, though one anesthesiologist you happen to run into in a bar waves you off a highly recommended orthopod, saying he had just seen the doctor butcher some kid's knee. The next best people are the physical therapists, and several you interview give you a name—Ted Firestone. Firestone is young, strong, and aggressive, your wife says he has the bearing of a quarterback. He guesses your surgery will take a couple of hours, but when it lasts for six, your wife gets worried. In addition to the replacement, he has to chisel out the old hardware, drill out the old screws, chip away the old growth, and repair your femur where it has cracked. He had warned you that something like this might happen. When he first looked at your X-rays, he said two things: your situation is beyond the abilities of most surgeons, and that surgeons in your past did you no favors.

You have recently seen one of your old surgeons, the doctor who hammered in your first nail, the doctor who told your father that with or without surgery, you would probably end up in a wheelchair by the time you are thirty anyway. It is the seventy-fifth anniversary of Crippled Children's Hospital, and they ask you to come speak. The doctor is old, old, old. In your speech you talk about the first time you came to the hospital, and then you single out the doctor, and give a list of things his nail survived; the car accidents, the years at sea, a body-slamming dance craze, a spectacular fall down a marble staircase, a crash landing in a realtor's plane, and in the end, you never mention those terrible words he said to you and your father that day, instead you thank him that soon you will be able to walk your sister down the aisle on her wedding day, the same little baby your mother sat in the car nursing the day you arrived for admittance to Crippled Children's.

While you are recovering, your hospital phone rings and it's some Hollywood producers. Apparently, the script you wrote for Altman has been circulating, and they want to know if you want to write for their TV show. You have to tell them that you don't watch TV and are unfamiliar with their show, and they say, *Perfect*. Come to Beverly Hills tomorrow for the interview if you want the job. You call an agent, and she says you should take the meeting, she tells you how much a job like that pays, and you misunderstand, you think the pay is what you make in a month, when in fact it's what you would make every week. You tell the agent there's no way you can get from the hospital bed in Scottsdale, Arizona, to Beverly Hills, you'd have to go into the meeting pushing a walker, and the agent screams, *For God's sake, don't go into the meeting pushing a walker!*

Your surgical nurse hears all this, and she is a big fan of the show, so she brings in some crutches, and your wife brings you a khaki suit, and they dope you up and get you on a plane. You are met by a special medical station wagon that takes you to the Beverly Hills address. Unfortunately, you have to climb about a hundred steps of exquisite, hand-cut, mossy California quarry stone from the curb so that by the time you get to the door, you have sweated completely through your khaki suit, and you have popped so many pills you don't remember the interview, but the producers hire you anyway, and that is your first job in Hollywood.

You have your other hip replaced right before you begin work on a medical drama. The showrunner is making a movie about F. Scott Fitzgerald, and your offices on the Fox lot are in the same building where Fitzgerald had his office long ago. The showrunner brings Fitzgerald's aged secretary in one afternoon, and she walks around telling you and the showrunner the history of the place. Toward the end, she passes your office and says, *And that was Billy Faulkner's office.*

BY THIS TIME YOU HAVE TWO SONS, the older of whom has a glitch in his spine. You are now the parent your father was, driving him to special clinics, watching as the doctors make him run, walk, stand on one foot. No one seems to know what the condition is. They think it's developmental and not degenerative, but they're not sure.

You tell your mother that you need some prayers sent your way. Your mother has been employed at the same hospital these last thirty years. She has worked her way up from switchboard operator to one of the managers in a terminal care ward of the hospital. People bring her their loved ones who are dying, and she sees that they are comfortable to the end, sees that they have what they need. Your mother has developed a network of prayer warriors at the hospital, mostly black women and a few black men who meet informally in side hallways and unused rooms to hold hands in a circle and offer up prayers. Your mother attends Bible study classes in the black part of town. On Sunday mornings, she attends her small white Episcopal church, and in the afternoons she attends her black friends' church, House of Prayer No. 2.

The situation with your son is a test of your faith. The platitudes you hear don't help. You do not offer platitudes to people in their times of need. You have learned that the only platitude you can offer others in a time of need is to tell them that you love them. You also do not offer prayers in the hopes of changing things. You have come to believe that those types of prayers are dangerous, especially when the word "if" is used. Those types of prayers are a type of negotiation, and you are beginning to believe that negotiation with God is sinful.

Your mother does not offer a platitude about your son. She recounts all the years of trials and suffering she says she watched you endure, and she says maybe all of that was necessary for you to be the parent of this boy who has his own difficulties. If that is true, then it is a kind of God's redemptive grace that you can finally accept.

ABOUT THIS TIME YOU GET A CALL FROM BEN, the priest at your church when you were a boy. Ben is retired and is a circuit rider to small country parishes that don't have their own priests.

Ben tells you that your father is dying in a small hospital down in North Carolina and he wants to see you. It's been about twenty years since your last communication with him, a single-spaced fifteen-page hand-printed letter dated *New Year's Eve*, in reply to a letter you had written months earlier. His letter is in the form of a multiple-choice questionnaire. Sample questions include "At what point in time did God die and you took his place?" and "Where in the Bible is it written that there is no place in Heaven for non-writers?" It is an angry questionnaire and your father closes it with a quote from *A Covenant with Death*, an out-of-print novel about a man accused of murdering his wife—*If you cannot love, pity. If you cannot pity, have mercy. That man is not your brother, he is you.* Your wife says you must go see your dying father, and she is right.

It's a small hospital in a small mill town like the one in which you grew up, and when you see the house where your father and his second wife live, it's the same three-bedroom brick rancher that is in your hometown where your mother still lives, the same bushes and trees and flowers planted in the same configurations. When you walk into your father's hospital room, he shoos every-one out and tells you to pull up a chair, he's ready to make his confession.

NO ONE IN THE HOSPITAL who knows you are your father's son seems to like you. Not at all. When you meet your father's doctor, the first white person you have met in the place, you ask him about your father's condition, what his chances are, and the doctor says, *Why don't you just make your peace and hit the dusty trail?*

Your father's wife is there and his stepdaughter, and they are perfectly nice. Your stepmother says she had thrown your father out of the house just before all this happened. He had wrecked his truck, drunk, and split open his head. He had spent a night in jail, making friends there telling jokes in his orange jumpsuit.

At his bedside your father says he wants to talk himself to death. He says he's ready to die, what do you think about that? Before you can answer, he says, *Everything is could have, could have, could have.*

They start giving him morphine. You ask him if his pain is specific or general, and he says, *It's endless.*

He asks you if you remember taking the St. Francisville ferry across the Mississippi with your grandfather, and you have a vague recollection of bright light on shallow water and watching your father and his father eat shrimp and drink beer in a place on pilings where you could see the river between the floorboards, and then your father starts talking about you as if you were someone else. He says you turned out all right in spite of it all. He says he can't figure out what made him trip off the end of the dock. He looks at you and asks, *Are you me?*

You tell him your name. You say you are his son.

Who is that grey-haired man standing in the corner of the room? he asks you, and you don't turn to look, because you know there's no one there. *There's a cat in the room*, says your father, *I can hear it.*

⁂

YOU TAKE A ROOM at a motel across the street from the hospital. Often when you go over, your father is sleeping. When he's awake, you're careful to let him spend time alone with his wife and stepdaughter. A black nurse finds you leaning against a wall in a hallway staring at your shoes. She tells you to be sincere in your forgiveness and walks on. When you see your father again, he says he's down to the bottom of the deck.

When your father is lucid, you ask him about all the work he did on the lake property. He says the black man who sold him the lake property feared retribution if he allowed your father to build an access road through his property. That's why your father hired so many local black workers to help him, the black stonemason who built the beautiful wall that was the only landmark on the lake for years. When the black road contractor lost the bid to pave the road, he wanted to see the numbers of the winning bid. As your father tells you this story, he begins to search through the top sheet on his bed looking for the paperwork from forty years before. *Save all these bits of paper*, he tells you; he says he wants to read the history later. When you try to ease out the door, he says, *Nobody likes to be left out, is what I'm trying to say, please?*

YOUR FATHER IS DYING, and he is angry with his own father. He tells you a trip to his father's grave affirmed all the hunches he's always had, but he won't say about what. He says he had a little room off the garage to build his radios and his father took it over to work on his clocks. Your father is getting himself agitated. His wife says for him to think of a quiet safe place, and he settles down. You ask him what place he's thinking of, and he says it's a stand of bamboo in the back corner of his house where he used to hide when he was ten years old.

One morning you go to the hospital, and there's a rush of people in and out of his room. Your father says he's going, right now, call a priest. You ask a nurse to call the local Episcopal priest as you and your stepmother try to comfort your father. A little while later a large black man in vestments comes in, and your father rallies to ask, *Who the hell are you?* There's been a mix-up; the nurse called the African Methodist Episcopal church by mistake. The pastor says he can still pray for your father, and your father tells him to get out. Your father's anger rejuvenates him, and it's good to see. Now the pastor is angry, saying that maybe your father could at least pray for all of us, since people close to death are closer to God, and your father refuses to pray for anyone, and you can tell that if he had the strength to get out of bed and bum-rush the pastor out the door, he would.

You get ahold of Ben, and Ben comes as quickly as he can. Your father is glad to see him. With you standing there, he tells Ben that it's going to be hard to say goodbye to you this time. He says you're a lot like him and that's what scares him. Your father apologizes for not dying. He says he got his times mixed up.

Your father slips deeper and deeper into the morphine. The last night you remember having a conversation with him, the movie *Carousel* was playing on the overhead TV with the sound off, and your father was watching it intently. He motions for you to come over, and when you do, he whispers, *Who are those two men folding that shroud in the corner?*

After that your father sleeps and sleeps. You go across the street to a funeral home and make arrangements with the undertaker. Your father has said he wants his ashes to be scattered offshore of the Outer Banks. The undertaker has just installed a new crematorium; your father will be the first to go through it unless someone else dies in the next day or so. The undertaker tells you about a sixteen-year-old boy who was just visiting two weeks before on a school trip, the teacher wanted to show the students what life on the streets could lead to, and at that time the sixteen-year-old boy had laughed the loudest when they toured the embalming room, and now the sixteen-year-old boy is in the back on the table himself, draining.

YOUR FATHER HAS BEEN ASLEEP for two days and two nights; you don't know what to do. You have a feeling that they will keep upping the morphine drip until it's over. You've been there two weeks. He may never wake up.

And then you get a call from Melvin. You haven't spoken with him in months; he says he has just had you on his mind, how are things in California? You tell him you are actually in Rocky Mount, North Carolina, where your father is dying. He says he's on the interstate driving home from Greensboro and he's coming up on the Rocky Mount exit with the blue hospital sign, and in about ten minutes he meets you in the hospital lobby. Long ago you have stopped believing in coincidences.

Melvin takes a room in your motel, and he has a quarter of a plastic bottle of bourbon, and you and he finish it and go out to dinner at a chain steak house, and you tell him all about what's been going on and what's been said these last two weeks. At the end of dinner Melvin says he thinks it's time that you went home

to your family, and you both later realize that that is the supernatural permission he had come to give you, though neither of
you know it at the time.

In the morning Melvin goes up to the hospital room where
your father sleeps and helps you rouse him. You introduce Melvin
to your father, and Melvin leaves to let you say your goodbyes,
and Melvin says later that your goodbye was awfully fast, that it
was almost as though you were following him out the door into
the hall.

You follow Melvin to his home in Virginia Beach, and you
cook a big pot of gumbo for his family and leave it to simmer, and
then you go down to Sandbridge Beach, way past the cottage
Melvin saved you from before, you go down to the preserve where
you had taken the girl from California on a break from handing
out campaign literature and you had seen a red fox with a bushy
red tail and had taken it as a sign that you would marry her, and
you go out on the empty beach, and a couple of miles down you
find the keel spine and wooden ribbing of an old shipwreck that
a nor'easter has thrown up on the beach. From where you are to
Hatteras south they call it the Graveyard of the Atlantic; there are
over six hundred shipwrecks out there, and this is not unusual.
The next storm will take the wreck back out again.

You sit, and you are very tired, and you try not to repeat the
Rolltop Mantra of being disappointed in yourself. You worry a
hand-hewn wooden peg from a joist on the keel of the wreck and
put it in your pocket and start to walk away, then feel superstitious
about taking it, so you walk back and kick the peg back into place,
and the next night you are sleeping soundly at home in your bed

with your wife and sons in California. You had said goodbye, and when he had asked, *So, this is it?* you had said, *This is it*, and when he had offered up his hand, you had taken it and shaken it and put it back in the folds of his sheet.

BEN'S GENERAL PHILOSOPHY IS people are generally doing the best they can. He tells you this as you wait for a Wanchese charter boat to take you through Oregon Inlet to the ocean buoy beyond, where you will scatter your father's ashes off the Outer Banks per his request. You talk about your father and his famous anger. Ben says he may have inadvertently angered your father when your father appeared one afternoon at one of Ben's little parishes with his next wife-to-be and insisted Ben marry them on the spot. Unprepared but willing, Ben cast around for a witness and was only able to enlist a handy black janitor. Ben says your father fumed and didn't call him for years.

You tell Ben how you had adopted the Rolltop Mantra to defuse your father's anger after the aquarium incident. The thermostat on your father's beloved aquarium went on the fritz, and your father kept turning the heater up and up until the neon tetras and black mollies and guppies leaped out of the hot tank, landing in little gummy blobs on the dining room floor. While cleaning out the aquarium in the kitchen sink, your father saw a much smaller boy give you a thorough whupping in the back-yard. Tapping on the window with his class ring, he summoned you inside. Your father shook some water off his fingers, landed a flying tiger across your face, then went back to rinsing the aquarium. You learned that whenever your father summoned you, especially to stand next to his rolltop desk, where a hundred cigarette butts smoldered in a large glass ashtray, you could re-cage the tiger simply by reciting, *I am very disappointed in myself.*

You rent a beach house for yourself and your wife and your two young sons, none of whom will be going on the charter boat. The morning of tending to your father, you go into the ocean alone at dawn, just when the convenience-store posters say not to, reminding people about the two fatal shark attacks that have recently happened just north and south of where you enter the water. AVOID SWIMMING ALONE AT DUSK OR DAWN IN A RISING TIDE. You make it out past the double sandbar, feeling the edge of a rip current so strong at one spot that it's as if your legs are tangled in sheets. The waves are confused but insistent. They keep coming—their nature, their job. You swim and then try to make it in without dislocating either of your two new hips.

Your surgeon would not approve of this. Even with the two new hips you are still in the habit of looking down so as not to trip. You have always hated the way you walk. Once, walking with your wife, holding hands on a boardwalk, she said to look down and see your shadows together, and you refused. You won't watch the reflection of yourself approaching storefront windows. A friend, possibly the boy from college with the melted face, said it wouldn't be you without the way you walked. He said it's as if you're wading through something no one else can see. You stagger up onto the beach, find your towel, and wonder if that noise you heard was a sonic boom from Oceana Naval Air Station to

the north or something else. With several pounds of titanium hip
and femur in your body, you're cognizant of lightning. You're
the first off the beach when thunder rumbles. When you lived
in Virginia Beach that summer in the rich girl's attic, a beautiful
black-haired girl who rented boardwalk bikes and always wore a
long one-piece bathing suit was split open down her chest when
lightning found the zipper there.

Like Sam McGee happily sitting in the flames of the wrecked
barge *Alice May*, you have considered cremation, as you can never
be too hot, though going to hell, as you are learning, is not a com-
pulsory thing to do, and in your mind you really don't want some
funeral director handing your sons a box of ash and molars and a
shovelful of scorched titanium parts.

Your father hated the beach, had sand issues, couldn't swim,
and, like you, was actually terrified of water. At age four, you fell
into a chocolate creek in East Texas. Your father stood beside
you, fishing, you don't think he pushed you; you were just the
type of child who accelerated the odds of inevitable mishap. You
stood beside water, therefore you fell in. Your father, unable to
swim, saved your life by lying prone on the dock and reaching
around frantically in the water until he found your shirttail. You
were landed, drowned, and resuscitated by a doctor's wife who
later bathed you in a sink and tweaked your erection to staunch
your crying.

Freud said storytelling is an unconscious desire to summon
fears in order to be able to exorcise them. Your firstborn son with
the twist in his spine accelerates the odds of inevitable mishap by
sheer proximity to slick floors, wobbly chairs, sharpened pencils,

hot stoves. You imagine him in these Outer Banks being sucked out by the notorious undertow, which has almost drowned all of your friends at some time during the last forty years. Stupidly surfing a big onshore hurricane break years ago, you got tumbled and spiked on your left shoulder, splitting the scapula in two. The doctor said it takes at least seven hundred pounds of pressure to split a scapula. Lucky it wasn't your neck, he said. But what are you going to do? Not go back into the ocean, ever? Freud also said the most important day in a man's life is the day his father dies. For now, you would suggest it's the day your first son is born. You were your father's only son, his firstborn.

On the day of the ashes, you quote Ben, loosely, the favorite collect that he used in services thirty years before—*Come, Holy Spirit, come, come as a wind and cleanse, come as a fire and burn; convict, convert, consecrate our lives for our great good and Thy greater glory*. Ben says he doesn't remember where it comes from. *Have you ever thought of the ministry?* he asks. You tell him about being talked out of it by the visiting Anglican bishop. Ben says the bishop must have thought you were a good writer. *Or else he was Satan*, you say. You ask Ben if he thinks they would have let someone like you into the seminary, and he says when he went through, he girded himself for what he had been told was the toughest interview in the whole process. He says his interviewer mainly wanted to talk about airplanes. When Ben asked him shouldn't they be talking about more serious matters, the interviewer said the main purpose of the interview was to comb for messiahs and homosexuals, and he could tell Ben was neither.

On the way out to where you're going to attend to your father, your sister joins you, and you and Ben spot a white disk, like a Communion wafer, and the disk hovers over the south end of the beach before slipping westward. Maybe it was one of those banners pulled behind an airplane advertising reggae and fish tacos; maybe it was something else. You can't tell, and neither can Ben, even with his Air Force eyes. The captain of the *Captain Duke* asks if you've brought a camera or flowers. You've brought neither. You have a tape with one of your father's favorite songs on it—a song about Lake Charles, the place of both of your births, but the mate says the tape deck hasn't finished chewing up the last tape they put in a while back.

Ben, in full vestment, begins when the charter boat captain, a Wanchese native and part-time preacher himself, cuts the engines after pushing his bow into the wind. The words come hard for Ben at the commending of the ashes; he knew your father as well as anyone could know him. Ben puts his hand on your shoulder to steady himself as the boat drifts a little, side to side, during the gospel. He pets your shoulder twice at the place in the service where you're supposed to lean over the rail and pour out the last mortal remains. You wonder about the particle density of the remains, the way they seem to stream straight to the bottom, only the finer specks leaving a ribbon of beige pollen-like dust on the surface that clings to the boat's waterline.

The rest is the ride in, your quiet sister grieving over the paucity of good memories, you reciting the Rolltop Mantra at the thought of allowing the twenty-year estrangement between you and your father.

☀

YOU AND BEN ORDER FRESH GROUPER SANDWICHES in the South
Nags Head restaurant where once you were Sven and where
sometimes over the years your father went looking for news of
you. *He's at rest*, Ben says of your father after you are quiet at the
table for a long time.

He's where he wanted to be, he says.

☀

THE BOTTOM OF THE OCEAN is dark and cold and roamed by
Pleistocene fish that science has forgotten. One night you and
Steve were culling through what had emptied from the tail bag—
scallops, fish, ballast stones, sand—and something jumped up
and ran to the rail, and you're glad someone else saw it. It looked
like a hairless monkey with webbing between its arms and body.
It hopped up on the rail and turned its head and hissed like a cat
through cartilage-looking teeth. It had been a strange trip already.
A submarine, spooked by the fathoms of cable strung behind your
trawler dragging its dredges, had surfaced in an eruption of ocean
the previous night off the starboard rail. Its brightening, pulsing
amber light lit the water from below the area of a football field,
signaling Everything Must Yield moments before the submarine
leapt like a giant fish, roaring and snorting ballast blasts of foam,
its bow wave nearly sweeping everyone off the deck. The crew
had been taking little white pills that flapped shrouds in the edges
of the deck lights already. The boiled-looking furless monkey
hissed at everyone on the rail again before diving overboard. No
one would have believed you if you had told about the monkey

thing, but there was a guy on board who said he had seen worse. He couldn't talk about it without tears welling up in his eyes. That's the kind of thing you find at the bottom of the ocean, where your father wanted to be.

The day after your father's ashes you take your elder son down to Wanchese. Wanchese was the bad Indian, your fifth-grade history teacher used to say, the one who turned against the colonists after they kidnapped him and the good Indian Manteo and took them to London. Returning to the New World, Sir Walter Raleigh's men repaid Chief Wingina's kindness of feeding the starving colonists by shooting him in the buttocks and then severing his head. Wanchese defected back to his own people. Manteo was named Lord of Roanoke. Not much has changed in Wanchese: the derelict cars, broken marine gear, old culling boxes rotting in the marsh; the fish houses, the old trailer on the canal where you and Steve lived. Your son notices how many stop signs have been knocked off their corners. Grocery store accounts are still kept in spiral-bound notebooks. You ask about the notorious captain who first hired you twenty-five years before. Someone says he doesn't know, maybe Alaska, maybe South America, *maybe sumwarz up norf.*

You take your son to the South Nags Head restaurant. It's been flooded a couple of times by hurricanes, an old picture of you and Steve long gone from the wall. You still know some of the women you knew back then who are still there now. They've married commercial fishermen once or twice, raising teenagers now; they say that your son looks so much like you that you must have spit him out of your mouth.

What is an apostrophe? your son asks on the way home. He's

five years old, and he further resembles you by walking with his
back bent a little forward, with the view of his feet that affords. At
the beach that week, he will find a watch, a piece of rare coral, a
Smith & Wesson tactical knife, and, in the ruined inner court of a
washed-over sand castle, a shark-tooth fossil.

You're often flummoxed by his simple questions. You work
through an unsatisfactory explanation of possessive mechanics
and contractions. Finally you tell him it's usually a little speck that
means something's missing.

The evening veil is on the Atlantic to the east even as Pamlico
Sound to the west is still lit like a lake of fire. As you drive north
to supper, you point out the cottage where his mother and you
stayed six years earlier, the kind of old shuttered place they're
now tearing down to build the eight-bedroom models. There's
a tiny bedroom in the back with a broken-shouldered double
bed in which he was conceived, beneath an old reproduction of
Winslow Homer's *Hurricane.*

You pass an old outdoor pay phone where you spent many a
midnight leaning into trying to make something right with someone miles away on the mainland. This is the place where your
father is cast and your son was conceived but it is not home. It's
a beautiful place but you tell your wife you don't think you need
to come back here ever again. This is a place where only God
knows how close you came to what *could have been*, and only His
grace saved you from it. It's the lesson of Shadrach, Meshach, and
Abednego in the oven of the insane king Nebuchadnezzar: sometimes God saves us through the fire, sometimes He saves us from
the fire, and sometimes He saves us not at all. If He doesn't save
all the special children, who does He save?

AND SO IT COMES TO PASS that seven years later you find yourself sitting in a hard wooden pew in a tiny whitewashed cinder-block church in winter with little heat, the one toilet is clogged, there's an outhouse out back if you're really in need, and the bass player is missing a string on his bass guitar. You and your mother are, as usual, the only white congregants in House of Prayer No. 2 on Pocahontas Street in Camptown. There is much praise and music and glad uplifted faces around you, but this day you remain seated, unmoved. You have been coming to this church for the last fifteen years when you are home. You know the regular saints, and the regular saints know you. This is not the kind of black church where, when white tourists show up slumming to listen to the music and to be entertained, they are seated in the hot seat of the front pew.

You doubt any white tourists have ever attended House of Prayer No. 2, at least not since you have been coming. There will be a couple dozen spontaneous hymns, a lot of personal testimonies, at least two collections, a sermon, and an altar call where many will be slain in the Spirit. Deacons of the church will stand ready to catch the slain and to cover them with blankets if they need to be covered. If you ask Pastor Ricks what happens when he lays hands on someone and he or she is slain in the Spirit, he says it's when the natural is *overshattered* by the supernatural, the person's overpowered by something greater than him- or herself and enters a sleep like Adam slept when God removed his rib. In that state there is a spiritual impartation, something changes in the person, letting him or her know the reality of God.

No one looks at you funny during a hymn; everyone else is standing and clapping and singing, you remain seated in your pew. The constant up-and-down is hard on your back and knees. There is no hymnal, and you only know a couple of them by heart anyway. Sometimes during the singing you sing, sometimes you sit and pray, and sometimes you are just sitting there looking at your watch, computing rental car return and security time because, with your metal hips, you will always have to be patted down at the terminal. The services at House of Prayer No. 2 usually run more than three hours, the nearest airport is an hour away in Norfolk, and often you have a Sunday night flight back to California.

When you stand and give your testimony during the time to testify, everyone probably knows what you are going to say; you are grateful for the prayers Pastor Ricks and the congregation send to you and your family in California, especially the prayers they send to help your eldest son with his physical condition, you are grateful for your prayer-warrior mother, and you are grateful for your relationship with Pastor Ricks, with whom you share your faith walk over long distance, the Holy Spirit a function on your cell phone, some days you can almost count down *three, two, one* when the phone will ring and it will be Pastor Ricks calling. When you tell him about your stumbling faith walk, Pastor Ricks listens and doesn't offer platitudes, he offers narratives, and it comforts you, even in his first words as he begins, *Well, you know, when Joseph was perplexed* . . .

ON THIS DAY YOU SIT on a hard pew and you are cold, and when you try to pray, your mind wanders to back taxes and sex, hardly the smoky burnt offering of prayer rising pleasant to the nostrils of God.

You had recently made one last run at the seminary, had asked for and received from Ben and from Will letters of recommendation, and had been narrowly accepted. There was a problem with your thirty-year-old college transcripts, and it was hard to explain to an admissions office person in Pasadena why you failed Sculpture 101. The woman teaching the sculpture course with the two little dachshunds that pissed everywhere in the studio had wanted a spike driven through a perfect ball of clay, and you had turned in Nat Turner hiding in a tree-root cave with his sword and the head of a child in a burlap sack, historically unsubstantiated.

On the eve of your first day of classes at the seminary, your wife had gone into labor and delivered naturally, without drugs, as she had with your other two sons, and the ten-and-a-half-pound third son's cannonball-sized head had split her pelvis. Shuffling through the house in a tightly cinched orthopedic corset, she, as well as your new son and your other two sons, was dependent upon you, and seminary would have to wait for at least two more years according to the cycle of when Hebrew 101 was being offered, a prerequisite.

You had returned to television writing and sought out a spiritual community in Hollywood, though the people you had met so far were more interested in television shows and movies in which people of faith protected souls by fighting teen idol agents of Satan, fire-breathing dragons, Muslim hordes, and supersecret cells within the government. The problem for you is that, like your favorite writer, Flannery O'Connor, you believe the biggest threat to your soul is *you*.

When you can, you come home to Virginia; you still think there is an untold story in the story of Nat Turner, whose skin you had once touched nailed upon the board in fifth grade. Lately in your town there has been renewed interest in Old Nat. The black community is talking about raising a monument to him as a counterbalance to the concrete Confederate memorial in the park. The white folks have answered, Are you kidding? The guy was a mass murderer.

One Sunday you are sitting in the church of Pastor Ricks, a man who, like Nat, is considered by his congregation to be a prophet. Like Nat, he has had visions in the clouds at night. In one vision, Nat saw black and white spirits in struggle. Pastor Ricks says he has seen a figure of Jesus so tall that the moon was a small white disk on His shoulder. In his vision, the heavens open, and all people on the earth are revealed to be worshipping this Christ, and in a dream Pastor Ricks has seen all people of all races and colors watching a movie, and he says he hopes one day it is a movie you will write.

On one Sunday afternoon, Pastor Ricks's sermon is from Genesis. Some Baptists you have known don't usually dwell in the Old Testament; they prefer the good news in the New Testament. You have found plenty of good news in the Old Testament in the stories and the people God has chosen to work His Mysterious Ways: Moses, *murderer*; Rahab, *whore*; Abraham, *wife pimp*; David, *adulterer and murderer*; Elisha, *slayer of children*. It is hard for you to place Nat's theology, though it must have been rooted in the Old Testament somewhere. In your research you have located his sword and the rope from which he hung before he was decapitated, skinned, boiled into fat, and cut into pieces. You have discovered that Nat and his confederates killed fifty-six white people in two days with mostly axes and hand tools, at one point slaughtering ten schoolchildren and their teacher and stacking their bodies in one pile and their dismembered limbs and heads in another. This may be a story that needs retelling, but it is not a movie that will ever be made in Hollywood, even with the slavery backstory and the third-act slaughter of innocent blacks in the bloody, retributive aftermath.

This Sunday you are sitting in a hard cold pew, and you wish you had the passion for Christ of the people around you. They are poor, and in their testimonies you hear of lives that are often dire. They are singing and clapping, and you are cold.

The sermon begins in Genesis, because this is a Pentecostal church and God resides in the Word. The Word that morning is Genesis 28:16 concerning Jacob—*father deceiver, brother betrayer*. You've always had a fondness for Jacob with his bad hip, have always had an ear out for what it might mean to you. You're familiar with his story—Jacob is the guy who stole his brother Esau's birthright by covering himself with lambskin to fool his blind father, Isaac. His mother put him up to it. When she saw that Esau was probably going to kill Jacob, she told him to flee and he did so, taking only his stick. Just before crossing the Jordan, he slept with a rock pillow, and God showed him the famous ladder to heaven, though it was probably terraced steps. And Jacob awoke out of his sleep, and he said, *Surely the LORD is in this place; and I knew* it *not*. A great negotiator, Jacob cuts a deal with God. Jacob promises to tithe ten percent of all he has if God will bless him on his journey to save his skin, being spun back at home as a wife hunt. And Pastor Ricks ties it in with Genesis 31:13, when the angel of God tells Jacob it's time to go home.

Pastor Ricks's sermon is about Jacob's spiritual beginnings, and how the world will try to erase your spiritual beginnings, and how sometimes it is necessary to go back to where one's spiritual journey began.

Pastor works the theme until he is certain the saints are understanding. When Pastor Ricks dwells on the message, massaging it just so, he says, *Let my coals burn in the fire a little longer, somebody tell me one thing*, and somebody usually says, *Tell it, Pastor Ricks*.

At the gathering of the offerings, a small wooden table is brought out, and pew by pew you file up with your money, and you see that most of the bills are dollar bills with an occasional five or twenty, and there is also plenty of change. Your mother says on the ride home how refreshed she feels, but that day your cold bones felt the time tick past. You remark to her from your small heart that you think you'll start tithing again so at least House of Prayer No. 2 can buy a decent space heater.

WHILE YOU ARE HOME, Pastor Ricks tells you about some land he's got his eye on that he's heard is selling for cheap, a possible tract to buy for a new church someday. He's been out looking for land like this for a while, and the bargains he sees listed are bargains for a reason. Some of the acreage is wetlands and some is in the floodplain. Your town has just had a five-hundred-year flood, water rising in the middle of town at six inches an hour when a hurricane stalled over the swamps to the north and west and the rivers full of rain and snakes spilled their banks so that downtown was under twelve feet of water.

You ride around with Pastor Ricks looking at land and see a sign for some riverfront acreage that is freshly bulldozed from the buildings the flood had ruined. You can probably get that land cheap; the owner is a man who is rich and has been known as benevolent in land giving in the past. It turns out that you can get the land cheap, though when you gently hint through back channels wouldn't it make a nice donation since a church will be built there, the price remains the same. City hall says you can build there, but you'd have to build a structure on pilings with a floodgate beneath. There's some property across the street from the church, but its backside runs down to the river as well.

You don't really see the need for a big new church. Some of the Sundays you've been at House of Prayer No. 2 there have only been a handful of people. A new church is a good idea for the future, a dream, a vision. When you get back to California, you begin to send your little trickle of ten-percent tithes to the place, hoping it will go toward getting the toilet fixed or that new space heater.

ONE NIGHT PASTOR RICKS GIVES TWO MEN a ride out in the
county, and one of them tells him of a church being built by
convicts, so Pastor Ricks goes out there the next day, and, sure
enough, inmates from a local prison in orange jumpsuits are
building a church. Pastor Ricks finds out it's a new program for
trustees with building skills—brick masons, carpenters, electri-
cians, construction workers—to work off some time in exchange
for their labor. All you have to provide are the building materials.

God honors faith, and even though he has no land on which
to build or money for materials, Pastor Ricks puts his name on
the prison's building list and hires an architect to draw up plans
for a new church.

None of this makes sense to you when you talk to Pastor
Ricks about it long-distance. When you call him and ask him
how he's doing, he always says, *We're still believing in God and
continue to look to the Lord for greater things*, except there's a
new excitement in his voice when he says it now. You're a little
worried. Pastor Ricks is an honest, godly man, and you person-
ally know some of the men who own some of the land he's been
looking at, and these men are worldly businessmen who would
not flinch at selling a pastor a piece of swampland for the price of
prime. But Pastor Ricks's faith is far greater than your own. When
he sees marshy vegetation on one tract of land, he calls the Army
Corps of Engineers, who come and take a soil sample and say
he's right, this land is prone to flooding according to the geologic
record.

You check in with Pastor Ricks every few days. He's had a setback: the county zoning won't let him build a church as large as he wants to build on any of the land he has found. That is when you suggest he build a church on the property his church already owns. It might be smaller than the church he had planned, but he might be able to adjust the blueprints to fit the church on the existing lot.

※

IT IS ABOUT THIS TIME that you are finishing writing a movie script about some Army veterans returning home from the war in Iraq. On the day you sell the script, you are pleasantly surprised at the selling price and neglect to thank God for your good fortune, and when you do get around to thanking God, you immediately remember your pledge to tithe ten percent of your earnings to House of Prayer No. 2, and the small heart in you cringes, wondering if that is ten percent of gross or ten percent of net.

You put off calling Pastor Ricks to tell him about selling the script, even though it would please him that prayers for your success are being answered. When you call him, he says they are still believing in God, looking for great things from the Lord, standing on the Word of God, but he's a little worried that the time is drawing near when the convicts will show up to begin work on the church. He is concerned that he doesn't have the money yet for the building materials, and that is when you tell him to start getting prices on pallets of brick and loads of lumber, you sold your script.

Pastor Ricks needs a building contractor, and he sees one at a gas station. The contractor's father lives across the street from the church, and his mother is friends with your mother. Pastor Ricks asks if the contractor would be interested in overseeing a church project, and he is; the contractor has moved back from Maryland where he had been building expensive homes and has had some difficulties. He has come home to be close to his father, who is dying.

You fly home, and you and Pastor Ricks buy A-frame supports for the roof and loads of shingles, and you start stockpiling tools the convicts will need. You are spending a lot of money, and the whole idea sounds crazy as you watch trucks off-load the materials that are now stacked higher than the little church they are set beside, so you don't tell anyone.

The contractor has looked at the blueprints, and he gives you and Pastor Ricks a figure on the blueprints, and it's a lot more than you can spend, but Pastor Ricks is not worried, he knows the saints in the church will donate, and all you think about is the tabletop of singles and fives and handfuls of pocket change.

THERE IS A GROUNDBREAKING CEREMONY behind the church one Sunday afternoon after service, and everyone gets a chance at the sledgehammer, and the first things knocked down are the old outhouses.

The bus from the prison pulls up one morning, and the convicts get out in their orange and khaki jumpsuits and begin the rest of the demolition. You have forgotten to get a Dumpster, so you rent one that the convicts immediately fill up, and then you have to go rent another. The Dumpster company only accepts cash, and you give it to them. More tools are needed, and you go and buy them: hand picks, gloves, shovels, a wheelbarrow. The prison program director says the work goes better when you feed the convicts something other than the white bread sandwiches and bottles of water they bring with them from the prison. They appreciate snacks too. So you go out to Walmart and buy cases of soft drinks and juices, and cartons and crates of snacks, and store them in the Sunday school house next to the church. You buy coolers and ice, and set up a fund to replenish the supply, and also calculate how much it costs to feed the busload of men daily hamburgers and pizza, and you set up a fund for that as well. When you get back to California, your lawyer tells you the studio is deferring half of your script payment against box office to finance the film, meaning you will never see that money after all.

Every couple of days Pastor Ricks calls you with an update. There are unforeseen costs and problems. The brick masons are so good they're about to run out of bricks, and you miscalculated how much brick you'll need, and you're writing a large check to a brick company.

You fly back home to Virginia, and you and Pastor Ricks go look at doors. You did not realize how much doors cost. There are the large ornamental doors for the front of the church, then there are the vestibule doors and the door to the new pastor's study, plus the side doors and the back door and all the emergency-exit hardware that has to be installed to bring the project up to code.

THE CONTRACTOR LOOKS WORRIED, and you think it's about
the project, and part of it is, and part of it is his dying father, and
part of it is the situation he's gotten himself into that requires
him to spend a week in jail. This puts the new church at risk with
the prison program. If there are no materials or oversight for the
convicts, the prison pulls them off the project and sends them to
another project somewhere, and you lose your spot on the list,
and your project can become an interrupted construction site
forever or at least a very long time.

You fly back to California and begin to deal with a studio
and a studio's notes on your script, which is set in Texas, and the
first note you get from the woman at the studio is that she doesn't
believe that men in Texas still wear cowboy hats, and from that
point on, the notes get worse. You think of the shortest sentence
in the Bible—*Jesus wept*.

Pastor Ricks is beginning to hate to call you, you can tell. Here
are some things that are costing more than planned—the wiring, the
heating, the air-conditioning, the oak trim, the carpeting, the light-
ing, and the new pews. Everyone is reaching deeper, Pastor Ricks
and his wife, you and all the saints. You are becoming downspirited,
and Pastor Ricks reminds you that anytime you sow godliness, you
will receive opposition from the Devil because the godliness you are
sowing will liberate someone from bondage; once you break through
the opposition, the blessings will flow, and in faith you must never
give up, because to give up means you will never succeed.

\\|//

SMALL MIRACLES BEGIN TO HAPPEN. Pastor Ricks watches the transformation in some of the convicts. He says some of the hard-core inmates soften and tell him they appreciate being treated as well as they are being treated on the job site, even if it is just a Walmart soda and a Little Debbie oatmeal cake. Pastor Ricks says during the day the inmates come around to the side of the building where he and the contractor are figuring the costs of the next day and ask Pastor if he will pray for their family members on the outside. For some, the closer they get to release, the more they worry about being accepted back into their families, they worry about what they will find when they get out, they worry about how they will react to what they find when they get out.

Toward the end of the project the police come around and arrest the contractor. He is charged with misappropriating materials from the state for his own personal gain. What comes out in court is that the contractor said he had been promised a bonus at work, and when his boss reneged on the bonus, the contractor ordered some paving material, paved some people's driveways, and kept what he charged them to do it up to the amount he says he was promised in his bonus.

This is not good. The church is only a few weeks away from completion, and without a contractor you have to hire someone and pay him real money, not the small amount you are paying the contractor.

This is something you do: You try to find the contractor's lawyer, and you make sure that he has retained a good one. Then you try to find out which judge the contractor will be appearing before. The judge is one of the sons of the Commonwealth's Attorney who grew up three doors down the street from you. Without calling him directly, you send word to him through back channels, begging for mercy.

At the time of the contractor's trial, Pastor Ricks delivers almost the entire House of Prayer No. 2 congregation before the judge as character witnesses. The judge remarks to you privately through back channels that he has never had the opportunity to hear so many character witnesses. He also sends word as to the minimum sentence the contractor must receive, and the contractor receives the minimum sentence, though he is immediately sent to a correctional facility and will miss the dedication of the new church.

You write to the contractor in jail and ask if he wants you to try to figure out a way to get him released for a few hours on dedication day, and he sends word through Pastor Ricks that he would have to attend the service in handcuffs and under guard, and he'd rather not have his wife and daughters see him like that.

�⁂

THERE IS AN OLDER INMATE from the prison who has built homes for celebrities and politicians in Northern Virginia, and one day he tells Pastor Ricks, *Preacher, I'm going to build you a steeple.* And he does, and it is beautiful—louvered, a hand-stamped copper roof, and a beautiful cross on top. He tells Pastor Ricks that he built it so that at some point a bell can be installed inside. Pastor Ricks says the man choked up when he said that of all the multimillion-dollar homes he has built over the years, nothing compares to the pride he has in that steeple. Pastor Ricks says it is the same with some of the other men who worked on the church, taking pride, making sure the details are just right, bringing their families by to see their work after they have been released from prison.

Pastor Ricks's wife gets a good deal on pews. She's found a church that is installing the more modern stadium-style seats, and she gets a good price on their old oak pews. The oak pews perfectly match the oak trim inside the church, the blue cushions perfectly match the blue carpet she also found a good deal on, furthering in her mind that the handiwork of God is to be seen throughout the church and its construction.

IT WILL BE A PACKED HOUSE the day of the dedication. You and your sons and your mother and your sister and your niece will be there. There will be many songs and there will be two sermons and Pastor Ricks will sing "Never Would Have Made It," and you will not have realized until now what a voice of quiet power he has. There will be testimonies and there will be congregants slain in the Spirit, receiving God's anointing sleep that He might heal them, change them, reach within them, so that they will awaken in a better place; Adam in the garden yawning out of his rib-robbing divine slumber, opening his eyes to Eve; Mary the virgin rousing from her chaste bed conceived with the Christ; Jacob the wanderer, a rock for his dreaming pillow, his feet finally set on the pathway home.

The man sitting in the pew in front of you will begin to shiver and to shake, and he will fall out into the aisle, anesthetized by the Holy Ghost. A deacon will come over and cover him with a blanket. Your Cub Scout middle son will lean into you and ask if you need to give the man first aid. It's just God at work, you tell him.

But for you, God's grace comes in the last regular service the week prior to the dedication, when there is still some spackling and painting to be done, when there is a ladder leaning behind the sacristy and a light hangs by its wires from a hole in the ceiling above the pulpit. That previous Sunday, Pastor Ricks's mother, Mother Ricks, a child of the Great Depression, is giving her testimony, walking and sometimes hopping in the aisle as the Spirit moves her. She says she is going to tell something she has told before, she is going to tell of a dream she had many years before, a vision, way back when. She says the elders of the church may remember the first time she spoke of it, and Pastor Ricks's sisters nod their heads, they remember. She says she had a dream of a time when the church would need to be rebuilt, and in her dream, a white man comes into their church and helps make it happen, and she says when she saw you first walk into House of Prayer fifteen years ago, she said, *Praise the Lord, it's him*, and with that, Mother Ricks lays her hand on your shoulder, and you, at last, are *slain in the Spirit*.

ACKNOWLEDGMENTS

The author would like to thank Mom, God, Jen for the boys,
George Parker for being a brother, Adam Atlas for being a cousin,
Nan Talese for the patience, Denise Shannon for back-watching,
Dr. Ted Firestone for the excellent carpentry, Casey and Denise
for the tax and trombone loan, Jim Dees for being cool, the
very benevolent Geoffrey Wolff, and these truly holy men of the
cloth—the Very Reverend Ben Duffey, the Very Reverend Canon
Robert W. "Father Bob" Cornner, Pastor Charles Stanley Ricks,
and the Reverend Dr. Ira D. Hudgins, aka The Preacher.

Visit Pastor C. S. Ricks and the saints at House of Prayer
Holiness at www.hopchurchinc.com.

ALSO BY MARK RICHARD

CHARITY

With *Charity*, Mark Richard again secures the distinction of poet laureate of the orphaned poor, the broken, the deceived, and the unrelieved. In stylistic brilliance, he renders their conditions with grace and compassion, and redeems and transports their tragedy with wicked humor. In the much-anthologized "The Birds for Christmas," two hospitalized boys beg a night nurse to let them watch Hitchcock's classic thriller film on television, believing it will relieve their Yuletide loneliness. "Gentleman's Agreement" is a classic father-son story of fear and the violence of love. In "Memorial Day," a bayou boy learns the lessons of living from Death himself, a fortune cookie–eating phantom who claims to be "a people person." From charity ward to outrageous beach bungalow, Richard visits the overlooked corners of America, making them unforgettably visible.

Fiction/Short Stories

ALSO AVAILABLE:

Fishboy
The Ice at the Bottom of the World

ANCHOR BOOKS
Available wherever books are sold.
www.randomhouse.com